THE QUEST FOR KIBI

White Orchid Books

THE QUEST FOR KIBI
AND THE TRUE ORIGINS OF JAPAN

Michael S.F. Gorman

with photographs by

Akio Nakamura

Orchid Press

Bangkok 1999

Michael Stuart Frederic Gorman (b. 1944)
THE QUEST FOR KIBI
Photographs by Akio Nakamura (b. 1932)
First published 1999

Orchid Press
98/13 Soi Apha Phirom, Ratchada Road
Chatuchak, Bangkok 10900, Thailand

Cartography by Meridian Mapping

The proceeds from this publication have
been donated by the author and Mr. Akio
Nakamura to the Oyama Foundation in
Kurashiki City to benefit international
exchanges for handicapped children.

ISBN: 974-8299-22-8 (HC)
ISBN: 974-8299-23-6 (TP)

MESSAGE

As a Kurashiki citizen with ancestral connections with the Soja-Kibi region, I am particularly pleased to learn of the publication of Michael Gorman's book *The Quest for Kibi*.

It is appropriate that this publication coincides with the twenty-fifth anniversary of the first sister city link between Japan and New Zealand (Kurashiki and Christchurch) which Mr Gorman initiated.

The magnificent plates of Akio Nakamura, one of Japan's leading photographers, will, I hope, increase international awareness of this fascinating and beautiful part of our nation, the history of which is complex and little known outside Japan.

It is generous of the author and photographer to donate their royalties to the Shigeki Oyama Foundation for use in international exchanges for handicapped children.

Shigeki Oyama (1905-1995) was a great civil benefactor and mayor of Kurashiki City. His efforts to establish international friendship have benefited so many people over the years.

内閣総理大臣
橋本龍太郎

Ryutaro Hashimoto
Prime Minister of Japan, 1998

FOREWORD

I remember discussing Kibi with Michael Gorman during my first visit to his home in Kurashiki a number of years ago. Sites, names, artifacts, legends, facts and fictions were all at his fingertips and were sorted out with remarkable clarity. It was, and has remained, a topic of almost passionate interest to him that we have enjoyed exploring over the ensuing years. Little did I realize at the time that his diligence in this pursuit would result in *The Quest for Kibi*.

Mr. Gorman has tackled a thorny problem that has occupied the attention of a variety of scholars for years. *The Quest for Kibi* differs from past explorations of this topic in that it presents primarily ideas and opinions Mr Gorman has formulated through his study over the years. Mr Gorman may be criticized on the lack of what academics will consider to be the proper support materials that often accompany such studies. But he should also be praised for the clarity and depth of his understanding of the accompa-

nying issues that surround the history of Kibi. The solution to a problem seldom begins with a footnote. Oftentimes the presentation of ideas and opinions, pure and simple, is the most difficult of tasks. In this Mr Gorman enjoys considerable success in making order out of confusion. The myriad of misinterpreted names of people and places, the unreliability of dates and relationships, the questionable accuracy of historical records, all are clearly presented and dealt with in this study, in an effort to provide some structure on which to build. *The Quest for Kibi* fills not only a vital need in this respect, but will also provide much material for future debate and consideration. For this, as well as the significant information set forth in *The Quest for Kibi*, Mr Gorman deserves all of our thanks.

Donald A. Wood, PhD
Curator of Asian Art
Birmingham Museum of Art, Alabama, USA
December 1997

CONTENTS

MESSAGE Prime Minister Ryutaro Hashimoto   v
FOREWORD Donald A. Wood, Ph.D.   vi
TABLE OF PLATES MAPS AND CHARTS   ix

INTRODUCTION   xiv

CHAPTER I THE DAWN   1
    The Early Kingdoms   3

CHAPTER II THE YAYOI PERIOD AND TOMA   5
    Japan's Earliest Paddy Fields   6
    Farming and Hunting   9
    Stone, Iron and Bronze   10
    The Inland Seaway   12
    Clues from Swords   15
    The Mystery of the Tablets   17
    The Dotaku Masks   18
    The Magical Powers of the Fundo   19
    Where was Toma?   20
    Kibi in Late Yayoi   21

CHAPTER III THE EMERGENCE OF THE KIBI ROYAL FAMILY   25
    The Tumulus Connection   26
    The Story from the Graves   27
    Kibi and Haniwa   27
    Graveyard of the Kings   29
    The Palace of the Gods   31
    Prince Kibitsu-Hiko   35
    Two Views of Prince Kibitsu-Hiko   41

CHAPTER IV LORDS OF THE SEA   43
    Tombs by the Sea   45
    Monuments of the Inland Kings   50
    The Chieftains of Oku   53

Kibi's Iron Grip   56
Relations between the Kibi Royal
    Families and the Yamato Court   58
The Archaeological Evidence   60
Princess Kuro of Kibi   62
Sakitsuya, King of Kibi by the Sea   63
Tasa, King of Eastern Kibi   64

CHAPTER V SUNSET AND A NEW FAITH   67
The Demon's Castle   74
The Demon Dies   76
The Puyo and Kaya People in Kibi   83
Achi-no-Omi, Prince of Han   86
Yamato Centralizes on Kibi   90
Tatami, Coffins and Cremation   94
The Soga in Kibi   101
The Arrival of Buddhism   101

GLOSSARY   113
BIBLIOGRAPHY   120
INDEX   121
ACKNOWLEDGEMENTS   125
BIOGRAPHICAL NOTES   126

PLATES, MAPS AND CHARTS

1. The mountain valleys of northern Kibi.
2. Modern reconstructed Yayoi Period residences.
3. Iron contents excavated from a Tumulus Period tomb.
4. A bronze dotaku bell, Yayoi Period.
5. A ceremonial flat bronze sword from the Yayoi Period.
6. Pottery fundo talismen, Yayoi Period.
7. A ceramic long necked jar with stand, Yayoi Period.
8. A ceramic tokushu-kidai stand for burial offerings, Yayoi Period.
9. A ceramic tokushu-kidai stand with storehouse attached, Yayoi Period.
10. The great Kibitsu Shrine in Kibi.
11. The reverse side of a Yayoi Period bronze mirror.
12. Front view of the great Kibitsu Shrine.
13. Sunset on the Inland Sea in Kibi.
14. The Tsukuriyama Tumulus, late fourth century AD.
15. Precious iron contents in a pottery domed box excavated from the Kanakurayama Tumulus, Tumulus Period.
16. Korean bronze horse shaped belt buckles, late fourth century AD.
17. A carved stone tomb screen from the Senzoku Tumulus, late fourth century AD.
18. Stones commemorating the union of King Nintoku and Princess Kuro.
19. Magatama beads from the Yata Tumulus, Tumulus Period.
20. Korean gold earrings from Kaya, Tumulus Period.
21. Iron armour in Kayan style, excavated from the Zuian Tumulus, late Tumulus Period.
22. Kayan inspired gilt bronze sword hilts, Tumulus Period.
23. A reconstructed peasant's dwelling in Kibi.
24. The walls of the Demon's Castle.
25. The view from the walls of the Demon's Castle.
26. The Kamadan (kitchen) at the Kibitsu Shrine.
27. The Tatetsuki ruins, Yayoi Period.
28. The Kameishi omphalos stone, Yayoi Period.
29. Enormous dolmen at the Joto ruins in Kibi, Yayoi Period.
30. Monolithic rocks marking a Kibi burial site, Yayoi Period.
31. The Paekche iron seven branched sword «kept» at the Isonokami Shrine in Nara, mid fourth century AD.
32. The Inland Seaway in eastern Kibi.
33. Pottery tokan coffins from northern Kibi, late Tumulus Period.
34. A stone sarcophagus in the Komorizuka Tumulus, late Tumulus Period.
35. A Sue stoneware pedestal jar manufactured in Kibi, sixth/seventh century AD .
36. A Korean gold figure of the Taoist philosopher Lao Tzu, sixth/seventh century AD.
37. A Korean gilt bronze Buddha. Early sixth century AD.
38. A Korean Paekche-inspired temple roof tile, made in Kibi, Asuka Period.
39. A Korean Paekche-influenced roof tile made at the Hoita Kilns in Kibi, Asuka Period.
40. The misty hills of Kibi.

Maps
1. Korean and Japanese "Wa", 4th century AD
2. Topography of ancient Kibi
3. Topography of Kibi in 1998
4. The River Deltas and the Tumuli of Kibi, 4th - 5th century AD

Charts
1. Tumulus construction on the five Kibi River Deltas, late 4th - 5th century AD
2. Ancient chronology

"From the outset of my study of the early history of Kibi, I found it difficult to understand that, from the Yayoi to the middle of the Tumulus Period (400 BC – AD 250), at least two separate migratory invasions of the Japanese islands took place. These originated from basically the same area in the south of the Korean peninsula, but under very different political influences and climates.

The first invasions were passive and of a people primarily concerned with rice agriculture and trade. They brought with them iron and bronze which rapidly replaced the primitive stone tools of the aboriginal Jomon people.

. . . The second migration appears far from peaceful and although launched from much the same areas on the peninsula, involved an entirely different people from the far north. These were the Puyo, who, having trekked down the west cost of the peninsula from Manchuria and established the Paekche Kingdom, continued through to the southern tribes among which were some of the Wa kingdoms. The Puyo, whose origins were in eastern central Manchuria, among the fertile Sungari River deltas, were horsemen."

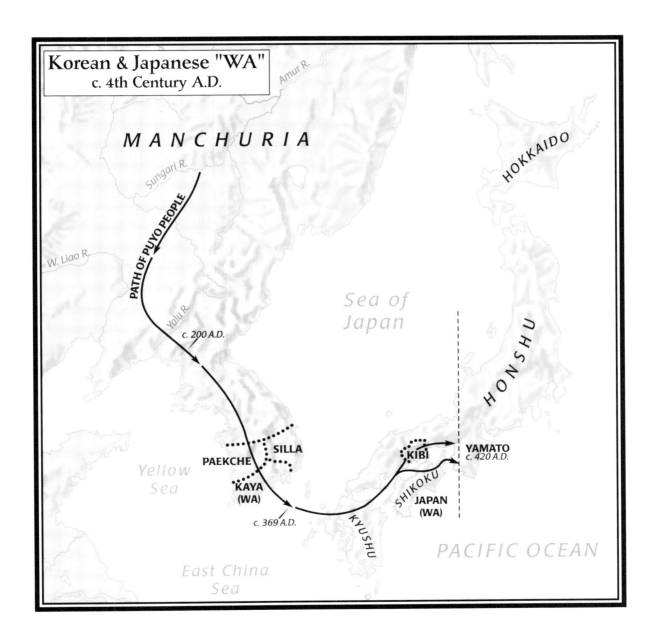

Korean & Japanese "WA"
c. 4th Century A.D.

MANCHURIA

Amur R.

Sungari R.

PATH OF PUYO PEOPLE

W. Liao R.

Yalu R.

c. 200 A.D.

HOKKAIDO

Sea of
Japan

HONSHU

PAEKCHE   SILLA

KIBI   YAMATO
c. 420 A.D.

KAYA
(WA)

Yellow
Sea

c. 369 A.D.

SHIKOKU

KYUSHU

JAPAN
(WA)

PACIFIC OCEAN

East China
Sea

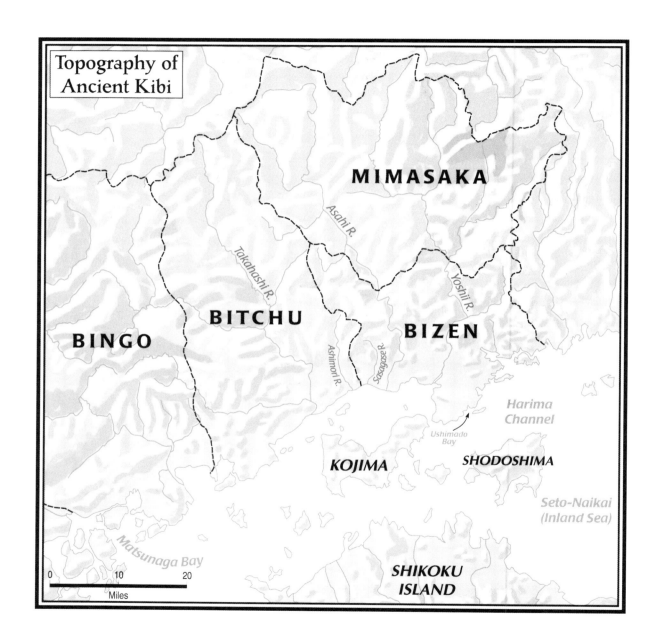

Topography of
Ancient Kibi

MIMASAKA

BINGO

BITCHU

BIZEN

Asahi R.

Takahashi R.

Ashimori R.

Sasagase R.

Yoshii R.

Harima
Channel

Ushimado
Bay

KOJIMA

SHODOSHIMA

Seto-Naikai
(Inland Sea)

Matsunaga Bay

0   10   20
Miles

SHIKOKU
ISLAND

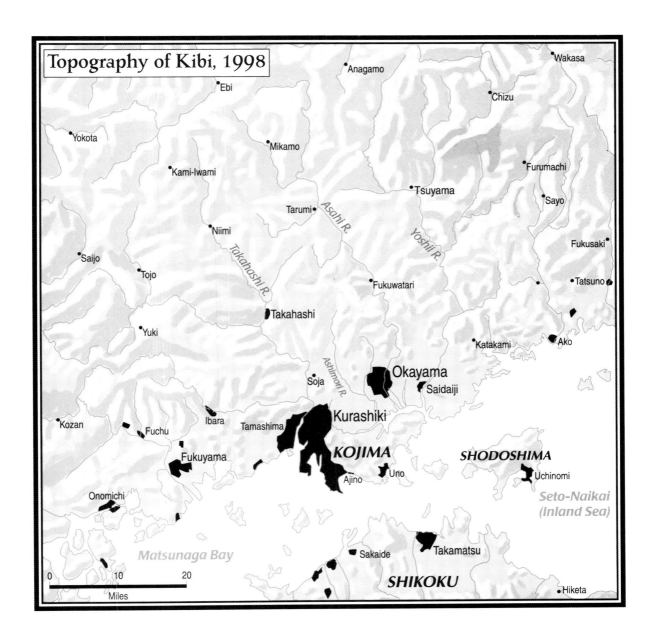

Topography of Kibi, 1998

INTRODUCTION

I first visited the ruins of Kibi in the late summer of 1968 and was immediately captivated by their rural setting. Then as now the rice paddies ran right up to the temple precincts. Farming communities nestled in the shadow of the tumuli, their blue and green roofed houses dotting the very slopes of the gigantic burial mounds. Finding few answers to my questions, I gradually came to realize that Kibi was a kingdom forgotten even by the people who live on the site of its past glory. Here had been the centre of a civilization so powerful that it threatened the Yamato court and was crushed. It must have abounded in palaces and placid canals and was possibly the cradle of Buddhism in Japan. Rich in temples and shrines, many of which survive today, these can be as architecturally distinguished as their better known counterparts in Nara and Kyoto. I was enthralled by the legend of the Black Princess and the stone sarcophagi which lie guarding their secrets in the tombs.

Kibi became a fixation but information was scarce. Few books had been written; I finally spent fifty thousand yen, a fortune in those days, on the complete set of Dr Nagayama's history of Kurashiki in twelve large volumes. I found to my suprise that none of my Japanese friends could read it, for it had been written in the early twentieth century in a style of Kanji now obsolete. Frustration did not cease at that point. The Archaeological Museums in the prefecture were organized with little regard for chronology and I spent hours trying to establish where the Yayoi period finished and the Tumulus period began. I soon realized that the 'experts' were little better informed, and to complicate the issue curators and university personnel could take what seemed to be perverse enjoyment in adding to confusion rather than illuminating it. Nevertheless I slowly began to glimpse some order out of chaos and the jigsaw began to fit together, but in a quite different pattern from my original notions.

I read the *Nihonshoki* and the *Kojiki* (Japan's first written histories of the eighth century AD) from cover to cover several times, noting as I went every reference to Kibi. I realized I had been side-tracked by a complicated historical cover-up. Kibi had existed with fascinating Korean connections. They were recorded but disguised in such a way that on first glance they would not be noticed.

Following the Meiji Restoration, the newly-established Imperial Household Agency, keen to justify its existence and burnish imperial prestige, began to take an almost unhealthy interest in the ancestry of the royal family. In order to prove to all the unbroken line of succession from the Age of the Gods and the first King Jimmu (660 BC) to Emperor Meiji (AD 1868), the Agency set out to identify the graves of the royal ancestors. Little scholarly care was taken and in the bureaucratic fashion of the time, with scant regard for truth, those nineteenth century civil servants caused as much obfuscation as the historians of the eighth century.

Today archaeologists and historians in search of truth are hampered by the bumbledom of the

1870s. Even now, long after the imperial renunciation of divinity of 1946, the authorities tend to suppress or distort any archaeological evidence which might offend the accepted Shintoist tenets concerning the history of Japan.

From the outset of my study of the early history of Kibi, I found it difficult to understand that, from the Yayoi to the middle of the Tumulus period (400 BC – AD 250), at least two separate migratory invasions of the Japanese islands took place. These originated from basically the same area in the south of the Korean peninsula, but under very different political influences and climates.

The first invasions were passive and of a people primarily concerned with rice agriculture and trade. They brought with them iron and bronze which rapidly replaced the primitive stone tools of the aboriginal Jomon people.

The Chinese, who were familiar with the peoples and kingdoms of the southern tip of the Korean peninsula and the Japanese archipelago, referred to them collectively as 'Wa' – the lands of dwarfs. There was probably little difference between the peninsula 'Wa' and those on the archipelago, although it is quite possible that the former were a little more sophisticated owing to their proximity to China. Political upheaval on the peninsula in the third century resulted in greater numbers of immigrants settling in northern Kyushu and then moving slowly eastwards towards the large fertile Kinai delta in central Honshu. The movement and influence of the new settlers has become clearer through increasingly sophisticated archaeological research.

The second migration appears far from peaceful and, although launched from much the same areas on the peninsula, involved an entirely different people from the far north. These were the Puyo, who, having trekked down the west coast of the peninsula from Manchuria and established the Paekche kingdom, continued through to the southern tribes among which were some of the Wa kingdoms. The Puyo, whose origins were in eastern central Manchuria, among the fertile Sungari river deltas, were horsemen. They were ruled by a warrior elite and kept hordes of captive slaves. The Puyo advances took place during the political turbulence of the early centuries AD. They first moved to the south-west of Manchuria following the fertile river valleys. Their path led them on into Paekche, moving rapidly down the west coast of the peninsula to the south. By the mid-fourth century, they had conquered the peninsular Wa kingdoms and then, together with their horses and trains of slaves, they moved on to Kyushu, subduing the Japanese Wa in an easterly direction to Kibi – where it seems they met with fierce resistance from the powerful Kibi chieftains.

The eastward conquest of the Puyo is allegorized neatly in the two Japanese first histories of the eastward conquests of the first King Jimmu – grandson of the gods. As I stripped layer from layer of fabrication, I realized the truth of these words:

"Mortal men are ever wont to lie
When-ere they speak of sceptre-bearing Kings".

This book is the outcome of my many years' quest for the reality of Kibi. I hope it will help to place Kibi in its true context in the development of Japanese civilization.

CHAPTER I
The Dawn

Ancient Chinese historians tell us that long before the Japanese people could write—in fact before the country, as we know it today, came into being—there existed many separate independent kingdoms each ruled by a fiercely shamanistic priestess who exercised her mystical powers over a wild and unruly people. One of the greatest of these kingdoms was Kibi which encompassed all of modern Okayama prefecture, the eastern half of Hiroshima prefecture and bordered the Inland Sea. The soil was rich, the land was fertile and famed for its beauty through the ages.

What were the origins of Kibi? Why do we know so little about it? The Chinese characters used to write the name have been in use for over 1,200 years but their etymology is so obscure that their derivation is lost in time. The name has been likened phonetically to the Japanese word for millet but the ideogram is different, and it seems that since the name Kibi was first written down the characters used were in their present form. These first writings were in the *Kojiki* (AD 712) and the *Nihonshoki* (AD 720), Japan's earliest histories. The *Kojiki*, which is notoriously unreliable, is the first history, a compilation of the recollections of a sixty-five year old woman, Hieda-no-Are, who was gifted with a wonderful memory and the prejudices of her sex. She was ordered by the Empress Gemmeyo (AD 662–722) to dictate all she knew and heard to Ono-Yasumaro who had been commissioned to write it down.

The *Nihonshoki* is not greatly superior and is often at variance with itself, placing, for example, one Emperor's appointment to the throne seventeen years before his birth and another's birth thirty-six years after his father's death. Both these annals must be treated with great caution and it is only in matters concerning the seventh century and later that they are in any way credible. The earliest reference to Kibi in the ancient histories is in the *Nihonshoki* in the first section concerning the age of the gods.

Here reference is made to the birth of Kibi-Kojima from the union of the male and female deities. At the time of the early histories Kojima, the coastal area which is now a suburb of modern Kurashiki City, was an enormous island, see maps on pages xii–xiii. We can certainly be sure that the name Kibi was in use in the eighth century AD and it is quite likely that it was current as far back as the Tumulus period, in the fourth and fifth centuries.

After the establishment of a central Yamato state government in the late seventh century AD, Kibi was broken up into three provinces—Bizen, Bitchu and Bingo—though this may not have been its first separation; there is an allusion to a central division of Kibi in a chapter in the *Kojiki* concerning the Emperor Nintoku (AD 310–399). In the reign of Ankan (AD 534–535) the term Bingo is first found, while reference to Bizen Kojima is made in the *Nihonshoki*'s chapter concerning the Emperor Kimmei (AD 539–571) which also refers to five separate districts in Kibi. Again in the *Nihonshoki* concerning the Emperor Temmu (AD 622–686), the term Kibi is used; it seems, therefore, that the area must have been one identifiable region at that time. In AD 714, during the reign of Gemmyo, the *Nihonshoki* records that the district of Bizen was further subdivided into six parts and an additional district of Mimasaka was created.

After the Jinshin-no-Ran (Civil War) of AD 672, a central imperial authority in Yamato slowly began to take control of the individual regions. In AD 675 the *Nihonshoki* reports that the governor of Bingo caught a white pheasant and presented it to the emperor; as a result the labour force due in fealty from Bingo was sent home and an amnesty granted and declared throughout the new empire. Nevertheless, no sooner do the new district names seem to have become established than a lingering reference to local government in Kibi is found. It may be that within the Kibi kingdom and its own government, allowance was made for the independence of small districts which could explain the confusion. This certainly happens in other areas. For example, in AD 714, the year that the Mimasaka district was created, Tango was separated from the provinces of Tamba—in modern Hyogo prefecture—and Osumi was created from part of Hyuga-Miyazaki prefecture. In the previous year (AD 713) Dewa had been created from northern Echigo-Niigata prefecture, and a part of Mutsu-Aomori prefecture. This illustrates that the unification of the ancient kingdoms into the Yamato state was a slow and complicated process.

By the end of the seventh century AD, Kibi was divided into three districts which, with the inclusion of Mimasaka, later became four. This implies that the great Kibi kingdom was, by AD 714, completely controlled by a Yamato central government. That Kibi was a thorn in the side of the newly established Yamato empire is, as my writings set out to prove, of little doubt. Its last years must have been turbulent and the confusion found in the territorial nomenclature of the late seventh century AD and the antagonistic attitude to Kibi in almost all references found in both the early histories tend to support my theory that the new court wanted it forgotten and written out of history forever. This constitutes some of the mystery of Kibi.

The Early Kingdoms

One of the most interesting periods in the study of ancient Japanese history is that of the kingdom of Yamatai (not to be confused with Yamato) as described and named in the Chinese chronicles of Wei of the third century AD. In these extraordinary documents, detailed descriptions of Japan are given by Chinese travellers of the time; names are given to the many Japanese kingdoms, collectively known as *Wa*, 'the land of dwarfs', through which the ancient Chinese travelled. It is, however, very difficult for us to identify all of them, although some are described so accurately in terms of topography and distance that we can clearly see which areas are being referred to. Unfortunately Yamatai falls into the more difficult category. Its exact location and details concerning its great Queen Himiko, who is alleged to have unified Japan, are still obscure. I personally feel that Kibi and Yamatai could have been politically related. The two kingdoms may have existed at the same time along with Yamatai's mysterious vassal kingdoms of Toma and Fuya. Even the combination of Chinese and Japanese scholarship has yet failed to reveal the key to the Yamatai conundrum but the ruins of Kibi do survive. The period between the time of Yamatai and Kibi's division into four districts is about five hundred years. During this five hundred years Kibi was founded, flourished and fell. Its connection to Yamatai and its real origins may be found in the ruins. This period should not be treated as a fairy tale nor should valuable archaeological evidence be destroyed. When Japan, as one empire, began in the mists of the early centuries AD, Kibi must have been a very important kingdom, ranking with Yamato. Little of reliable worth has been written and left to us by the ancients and what archaeological work has been done makes this abundantly clear. History is often selective, but the omission or suppression of the role of Kibi in the early chronicles is one of Japan's great mysteries.

Korea at that time

Neolithic remains indicate that the early Koreans, like the Japanese, were greatly influenced by the Siberian tribes, Mongols and Manchus. The language was probably Altaic which gives a fair indication of a common racial origin with the people of north Asia.

Cord- or rope-marked pottery called Jomon in Japanese is found all over Korea but its frequent incidence in coastal areas points to an economy based on the sea. From folklore we know that the people were divided into clans or extended family groups. The clans were headed by a patriarch who ruled through *shaman* powers with animistic overtones. The early Koreans believed that objects in nature were controlled by spirits. Natural events were the work of these spirits, which also influenced the lives of the people. The sun was the prime spirit and associated with legends almost identical to the sun-goddess belief in Japanese Shintoism.

As seafaring people the Koreans would have known of the Japanese islands and many families or clans would have settled, intermarrying with the Jomon Japanese people. The ancient Japanese were also a racial hotchpotch with strong influences from the South Seas, which were linked by a stepping stone of islands through Okinawa, Taiwan, the Philippines and the Celebes.

These South Seas people brought with them a distinctive architecture which is still to be seen in the Shinto shrines of today. These buildings on stilts were storehouses which were later transformed into shrines for the gods and houses for the aristocracy.

The mixture of all these racial characteristics gives the Japanese a distinctive physiognomy when compared with their more Mongoloid Korean neighbors.

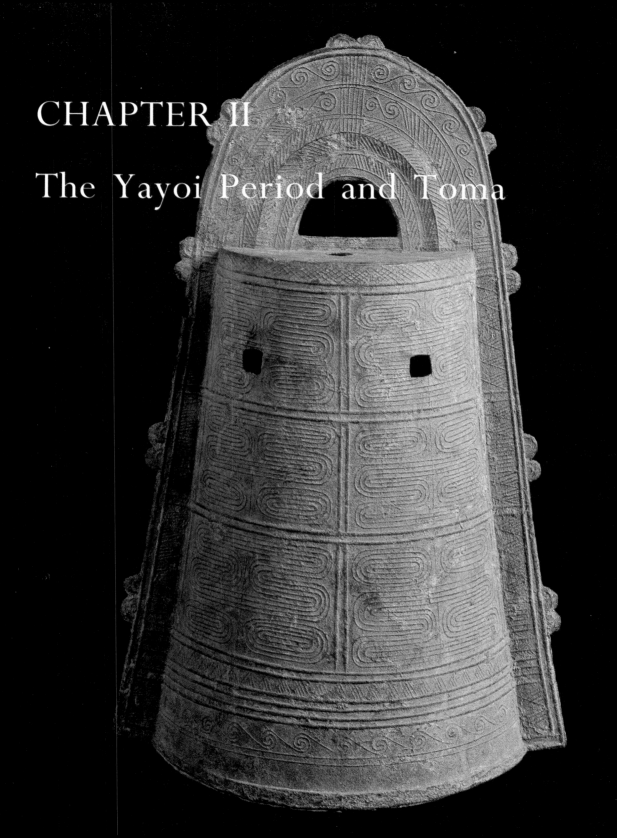

CHAPTER II

The Yayoi Period and Toma

Archaeologists suffer from the universal problem of having to struggle to preserve valuable historical sites from the ravages of urbanization. In the north of Okayama City at Izumi-cho is the municipal sports centre. In ancient times this area was known as Handayama and Ifuku. The sports centre lies to the west of the Asahi River with the Handayama Hills to the north. Until the end of the Meiji era (c.1905) this area had been used as paddy fields, but after the Russo-Japanese War it was turned into a military parade ground and used as such until the end of World War II. Shortly afterwards it was converted into a sports ground.

Over a period of hundreds of years the district was covered in layers of fine silt from the Asahi River and when, after the Pacific War, the sports ground construction commenced, some ruins which appeared to have been from the late Yayoi period (AD 100–250) were destroyed. The name of the site is Tsushima. Public opinion was divided between preservation of the site or continuation of the sports ground project. Unfortunately the prefectural government decided in favour of the sports ground, but not before concerned archaeologists had extracted from them a promise to preserve the area from further unsupervised excavation.

In 1968, plans were made to build a new stadium on the site to commemorate the centenary of the Meiji restoration. Even though the prefectural government was aware of the national law concerning the reporting and preservation of places of historical interest for archaeological study, and, in general, strictly enforced it on the public, it ignored the law in this case and construction was allowed to commence. Considerable amounts of pottery were immediately uncovered and much was destroyed. A delegation of Okayama's leading historians and archaeologists formally requested a halt in construction and reminded the prefectural government of its earlier promises, but to no avail. Piles were soon being driven into an archaeological site dating back more than two thousand years. Fortunately, however, the Cultural Agency of the central government was alerted to the danger, quickly examined the site and ordered construction to cease. Further damage occurred when amateur archaeologists from the Prefectural Board of Education started random and careless digging, destroying even more valuable evidence. When public outrage was voiced, the prefectural government, mindful of the Cultural Agency's authority, banned further amateur activity.

Japan's Earliest Paddy Fields

When professional archaeologists started careful and systematic work on the Tsushima site, they found that even though much had been destroyed by the piling, plenty of value remained. As a result of this act of preservation by the central government, it was discovered that here were the earliest rice paddy fields found to date in Japan; they are the key to a clearer understanding of the history of wet rice cultivation in the Yayoi period. Even though the rice paddies discovered at Tsushima were the earliest found, archaeologists are convinced that rice cultivation was introduced to Japan first in areas of northern Kyushu. It had been known, for some time before the sports ground location was discovered, that the Tsushima district was rich in Yayoi period material and, apart from this site, finds of the earliest Yayoi pottery and stone implements with ruins of dwellings had been found; these dwellings were in an area which in Yayoi times had been a small delta in the Asahi River affording the best conditions for wet rice cultivation.

During the millennium of the Jomon period (10,000–480 BC), which preceded Yayoi (c. 400 BC–AD 250) the Inland Sea had begun to recede, leaving large tracts of dry flat land and north of Okayama City the tributaries of the Asahi River brought down rich fertile deposits on which the early Yayoi people settled. Directly north of the Tsushima site at the foot of some hills can be found the Asanehana shell burial-mounds of the late Jomon period; from these mounds and the known burial practices of the earlier nomadic Jomon people, we can be fairly sure that, in late Jomon, the sea came right up to the northern hills and the area where the Tsushima site was found would most probably have been under shallow water. The Jomon people fished and gathered shells nearby. Over a thousand year period, from the beginning of late Jomon (600–400 BC) onwards, the landscape of Kibi changed dramatically; the confluence of the river water and the Inland Sea produced fine fishing grounds and where the Jomon people relied on the riches of the sea for their livelihood, the Yayoi settlers used the river water to cultivate rice.

We are still uncertain as to how or by which route rice cultivation was introduced to northern Kyushu by the Yayoi people who primarily came from Korea, but the new culture flourished rapidly all over western Japan. In ancient Kibi, Tsushima is believed to have been the first area where rice was cultivated, though the structure of these early paddy fields was quite different from those we know today. In the Yayoi period rice cultivation was a very uncertain living, for, in heavy rain, the young shoots could easily be washed away. Evidence has been discovered of the use of boards as a form of shoring the clay bank divisions between the fields. These were so placed that in heavy rain the rich top soil would not be eroded; this shoring must have been hard work, for the tools of the period were very simple and iron almost non-existent. From these first paddy fields we can understand some of the enormous problems which confronted the early Kibi farmers.

When the Tsushima paddies were excavated they were found to be in a remarkable state of preservation (no doubt because they were kept from the air); stalks, leaves and ears of rice were found exactly as they had been planted. Unfortunately, as soon as the plants came in contact with oxygen they discoloured so rapidly that there was no time for professional photography. Within the paddies many types of weeds were also found all combining to support prior archaeological theories on how early cultivation took place. The Tsushima site is of untold historical value and it is unlikely that such a fine example will be found again.

Naturally Tsushima was not the only area in Kibi known for rice cultivation in early Yayoi; in almost all the delta areas of the three great rivers of Kibi, the Takahashi, Asahi and Yoshii, small

1. The mountain valleys of northern Kibi, home to the northern chieftains. Many small communities dwelt in these valleys and developed cultural characteristics quite different from the coastal villages. Some were obviously very powerful because of constant mention of conflict in the early histories. In many cases the later northern tombs were filled with luxury items, although not constructed in the enormous style of the south. Iron deposits found in the river soil might well have been the reason for this apparent wealth.

settlements with their own paddy systems, have been found. Notable among these is the delta region of the Takahashi River which, in Yayoi, was near the present-day Ashimori River, now a tributary. The Iwakura site on this delta near the Sho suburb of Kurashiki City is particularly important as is, also, the Kadota site in eastern Okayama near Saidaiji and close to Bizen.

Some interesting early Yayoi settlements have been discovered in and around Kurashiki City lying in close proximity to Jomon shell mounds; quite often in this area, artifacts from the two cultures are found very close to each other. The Kurashiki suburbs of Fukuda, Shimaji and Funao are particularly rich in these cross-cultural remains. At Shionasu, also in Kurashiki, and at Shibukawa near Tamano City, which are both ancient coastal deltas, early Yayoi sites containing quantities of pottery and evidence of small paddies have been found close to Jomon period shell mounds.

Farming and Hunting

At Seno, south-west of Okayama City and at Kadota in the eastern part of the prefecture, early Yayoi shell mounds have been found containing the bones of animals. At the transition period, the burial practices and the two cultures were similar in many respects, the notable difference being the occasional small-scale attempt in Yayoi at rice cultivation. It seems fairly clear that at this time there existed two types of early Yayoi settlement; those on the coastal deltas appear to have been quite conservative, follow-

ing late Jomon practices as described above, while those on the more fertile inland marshes had paddies which were widened and improved without fear of tidal or storm damage.

By the middle Yayoi period, the coastal delta settlements seem to have disappeared completely, the inhabitants having moved inland to larger rice farming communities which were probably unsophisticated, peaceable and primarily concerned with subsistence from the land. From the archaeological finds the people seem to have had strong religious feelings, and to have been greatly occupied with magic and ritual ceremonies associated with rice agriculture and the technologies essential to its production.

Numerous early and middle period Yayoi settlements have been found around the eastern Inland Sea inlets of Kibi, on the large delta areas created by the three great rivers and along the Ashida River in Bingo in western Kibi. The settlements on the Asahi River delta, which were the largest, were spaced widely apart. On the river marshlands where the Yayoi people lived, large quantities of *ashi* reeds can still be found and the presence of Yayoi remains in the same area suggests that the early Yayoi settled wherever the reed grew abundantly. Along the Ashida River both the reed and Yayoi sites are found in some quantity. The early middle period Yayoi paddies were still not very well developed but the farmers do seem to have learnt how to extend the fields which were positioned in natural marshland; however they had not yet learnt how to harness the rivers for irrigation.

In the middle Yayoi period the people gradually began to position their settlements and pad-

2. Modern reconstructed late Yayoi period (200 BC-AD 200) style hilltop residences at Hinase Ushimado, eastern Kibi. These settlements were positioned with lookout advantages over the inland seaway. Trading vessels from Korea and Kyushu were constantly harassed by these coastal communities which prospered greatly from excise taxes levied on the sea traffic. This resulted in Kibi becoming rich and powerful.

dies away from the marshlands and some have been found on higher ground. This change naturally coincided with the beginning of paddy irrigation from the rivers—an improvement on the old reliance on the swampy river marshes. Some settlements have been found in small valleys which afforded ample irrigation from the many small streams which abound in the Kibi highland areas. One of the best examples of this later type of settlement on higher land is at Mt Abe near Kasaoka City in western Kibi where, at 400 metres above sea level, many ruins of middle Yayoi settlements have been found. Between Tsuyama City in Mimasaka and Miyoshi City in Bingo, in a row of valleys deep in the mountains, there were many villages, smaller than the old river delta communities, but greater in number. All were quite different from those of the Jomon people whose custom was to move from place to place in small nomadic family groups, hunting, fishing and foraging.

Stone, Iron and Bronze

Stone implements were still very much in use in Kibi in the middle Yayoi period; stone knives were used to harvest the rice and till the ground. The discovery of wooden shafts for stone implements has shown that iron was in use at the time but was considered so valuable that it was used solely for carving handles and blades for primitive wooden ploughs. At the Numa site in Tsuyama City in Mimasaka, northern Kibi, an iron tool called a *yarigana* was discovered. The Numa village is particularly interesting as it was disas-

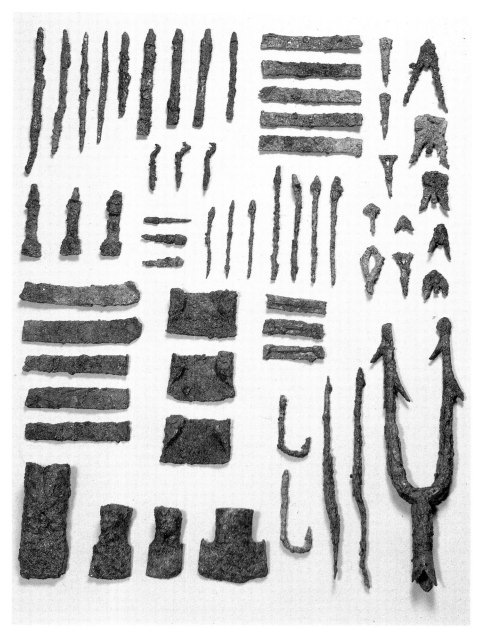

3. Precious iron contents from a pottery domed box excavated from the Kanakurayama tumulus thought to be the grave of a retainer of the chieftain or king buried in the enormous Tsukuryama Kofun. Tsukuryama Kofun is the fourth largest tomb in Japan and 360 metres in length. In the late fourth century, when these tombs were constructed, iron was still being imported from Korea in great quantity. The presence of such simple objects buried with such reverence indicates the importance of iron in the lives of the Kibi people of those days.

The Kurashiki Archaeological Museum.

11

trously and suddenly destroyed by fire, leaving many objects exactly as they had been placed before the fire. The *yarigana* or 'sharpening tool' was found in good condition, which is very rare. At nearly all other middle period Yayoi sites where iron has been found the tools have been practically worn out with repeated use.

How the Kibi villages obtained this iron is an historical puzzle. Since earliest historical record Kibi has been referred to as the centre of iron and this suggests the existence of an iron manufacturing industry which did indeed make Kibi famous, but this was rather later. In the middle Yayoi period it is unlikely that any local iron industry existed in the area. It is far more likely that the early iron implements were imported from Korea and therefore very scarce and valuable.

The earliest iron products and ore probably crossed the Genkai Sea from Korea and were first used in northern Kyushu. Later, the use of iron increased throughout western Japan and spread eastward as far as central Japan. Bronze also appeared first in northern Kyushu and spread in use in the same direction. There is similarly no evidence of bronze manufacture in Kibi in the mid-Yayoi period. From the number of bronze objects found in the Yamato district it is obvious that the volume of imports from Korea must have been huge in the context of the ocean-going ships of the time. Dependence on and trade with Korea must have increased greatly during this period and it seems likely that artisans, craftsmen and even merchants may have travelled with the trade and settled in Kyushu to arrange for the distribution of their products. So

few iron implements from the middle Yayoi period have been found that it is difficult to gauge the extent of imports but if the amount of stone implements found is any indication, then the quantity must have been enormous and even larger than that of bronze.

The Inland Seaway

In middle Yayoi times, the Yamato district seems to have advanced culturally and socially far faster than other regions. The bronze and iron for which it seemed to have an insatiable appetite travelled from Korea to Kyushu and then along the Inland Sea to its destination. Naturally the more imports this area required, the greater the importance the Kibi people attached to the sea-lane which passed close by them. In Yayoi times Kibi-Kojima was a large island and in its valleys many important middle period Yayoi sites have been found with the usual paddy systems similar to those on mainland Kibi. Trade goods from the Korean peninsula and the vessels which carried them must have passed between Kojima and the Kibi mainland. The importance of Kibi-Kojima in these early times is seen in its constant mention in the early histories; even in the eighth century AD it was still quite well known.

In Kibi-Kojima there are ruins of a village settlement away from the valley paddy systems 250 metres above sea-level on the top of a hill called Tanematsuyama. In Yayoi times most of modern Kurashiki city was under the sea. Until comparatively recent times there was a channel between

4. A bronze *dotaku* or bell discovered on Mt Tanematsuyama during the Pacific War. Bronze bells of this type are found in remote areas and were a Yamato stylistically inspired object. They obviously represented great power and were probably the possessions of chieftains. The decoration on the Kibi *dotaku* is related to the decoration on the ceremonial flat swords and the clay fundo tablets, which were unique to Kibi. The fact that Yamato-influenced *dotaku* and Kyushu-influenced flat swords are found in Kibi suggests that ancient Kibi was a buffer between two powerful clan groups in the east and west.

The National Museum, Tokyo

Kojima and the mainland which was sheltered and used as a safe anchorage in the storms which often hit this area. Another hill settlement to the east of Tanematsuyama, which is about 280 metres above sea level, overlooks Shodoshima Island to the south-east and the Harima Channel in the east. Many small islands lie directly south and it is obvious that these two settlements were fortified eastern and western lookout points which between them command views of the sea-lanes. At both these sites shell burial mounds have been excavated and at Tanematsuyama finds of fish hooks made from animal bones show that the people, although hilltop dwellers, went down to the sea to fish. The trading ships from Korea stopped at Kibi-Kojima for food, water and local pilots, and no doubt bartered iron and bronze for these necessities. But it is also likely that the lookout settlements would have engaged in piracy. Why otherwise would they have been sited away from food sources and water if they were involved solely in peaceful barter with the trading ships?

In many skirmishes with the Korean traders, the Kibi people may have been beaten and forced to retreat to their fortified villages on higher ground.

During the Pacific War a middle period Yayoi bronze *dotaku*, an important ceremonial bell stylistically derived via Korea from China and manufactured in the east in the Yamato region, was unearthed at the top of the hilltop settlement of Tanematsuyama. Considering that only a few hundred *dotaku* have been unearthed in the entire country, this small community must have been quite powerful and influential. On the north-west slope of the other hilltop lookout settlement a bronze spear, manufactured in the west, was found and between the two, on Mt Yuga, which looks to the south, a flat ceremonial bronze sword was also discovered.

These villages probably supplied the other Kibi villages deep in the northern mountains with their metals. Their importance is further emphasized by the fact that even though their populations were small by comparison with those of the inland Kibi people, more middle period Yayoi bronze artifacts have been found in the ruins on Kojima than elsewhere in central Kibi. The *dotaku* found on Kojima is of the earliest type and most westerly yet discovered. Finds of spears from Kyushu in the west and nearby an early dotaku from Yamato in the east suggest that in middle Yayoi the Kibi-Kojima district was important to both areas and a common meeting-point.

In Fukuyama City, in Bingo (now Hiroshima prefecture), there is a small peninsula called Numakuma where a further bronze spearhead has been found. The site is currently being studied and it is thought to be similar to the Kibi-Kojima lookout settlements. On Shodo Island east of Kojima yet another *dotaku* was found. The lookout settlements are not peculiar to Kibi, but have been found in Kagawa and Ehime Prefectures—in fact all around the Inland Sea.

By middle- late-Yayoi period the number of villages in Kibi had increased dramatically as also had the demand for iron implements, but by later Yayoi when enormous quantities of iron were being shipped from Korea and Kyushu to the Yamato region, the hilltop lookout settlements had disappeared. The use of stone implements was rapidly decreasing and the people were increasingly reliant on iron. Meanwhile, deep in the Kibi mountains, the late Yayoi villages were grouping together into a clan system.

Clues from Swords

A short bronze sword measuring 45 cm in length, 5 cm in width and 2.3 mm in thickness was found at Kumano-cho in Fukuyama City. It seems most unlikely that this sword was ever intended as a weapon—its use was probably religious and ceremonial. This fits the known practice of the northern Kyushu Yayoi people of converting foreign-made items to symbols linked to their own primitive agricultural society.

As we have already noted, from early Yayoi times rice culture spread from northern Kyushu throughout western Japan. With the early Yayoi archaeological sites very little difference is found from one area to another. But in late Yayoi great differences are found. The bronze *dotaku* culture which emanated from the central Yamato district differs greatly from that of northern Kyushu, which is characterized by bronze weaponry. The most striking differences in the cultures are found in the decoration and designs applied to earthenware pottery.

At this period, Kibi, and most of Shikoku and the other Chugoku districts, tended to follow Yamato influences in pottery shapes and decoration. The combination of the comb pattern with incised decoration which is almost unknown in northern Kyushu, yet abundant in Kibi and

Yamato, is probably the best example of Kibi's leaning to the east. The proliferation of bronze *dotaku* found in Kibi, compared with Aki further west in Hiroshima prefecture, again shows the Yamato influence. The fact that no *dotaku* have yet been found in Yamaguchi Prefecture, still further west, indicates that Yamato's power dwindled as it reached northern Kyushu.

Again in Shikoku this theory is borne out; in both Tokushima and Kagawa prefectures quantities of *dotaku* have been found, whereas none have been found in Ehime prefecture. It would seem, therefore, that Kibi marked the western boundary of strong Yamato influence, though it would be wrong to assume that the Kibi culture was totally dominated by Yamato. The very presence of ceremonial swords and bronze weaponry of northern Kyushu origin or influence suggests rather that Kibi acted as a buffer between the two powers and was culturally influenced by both, while maintaining its own unique culture and a certain aloofness. The finding of the *dotaku* and the ceremonial sword on Kibi-Kojima are significant in the light of this conjecture.

The presence of numbers of flat bronze ceremonial swords in Kibi introduces another puzzle. Away from the Inland Sea areas, this style has been discovered only in Oita prefecture in eastern Kyushu, while in northern Kyushu swords made in Korea and in other mainland areas are found in many late Yayoi burial sites. These weapons were also faithfully copied in northern Kyushu and traded eastwards. There is no evidence of the ceremonial flat bronze sword being manufactured in northern Kyushu and none have been found. It seems much more plausible that these

5. Detail of the decoration on a ceremonial flat bronze sword made in Kibi in the late Yayoi period (c. AD 1– 200).

Note the similarity in decoration with the Mt Tanematsuyama *dotaku*. These flat swords were for ceremonial use and may have designated rank. It is curious to note that almost identical decoration is found on bronzes manufactured in Yunnan, China, during the Han dynasty (200 BC–AD 200). These Yunnanese Dian culture bronze designs are followed through onto later Korean and Japanese *Sue* ceramics. See fig. 34. Artifacts from Yunnan have been discovered on islands north of Taiwan.

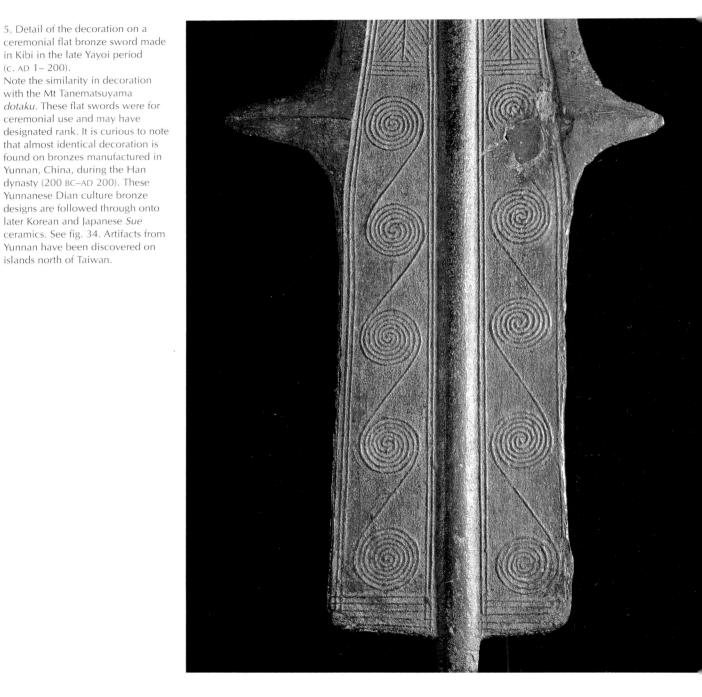

unusual swords were produced somewhere on the Inland Sea and that the directions in which they spread were influenced by Kibi.

They are found all around the Inland Sea and most interestingly also in Ehime—where there are no *dotaku*. These swords were considered as important as the *dotaku*, for they are often found buried together. The flat sword found at Mt Yuga on Kibi-Kojima had whorl designs on it identical to those often found on *dotaku*. The technology required to manufacture the ceremonial flat swords was not nearly as sophisticated as that needed to manufacture the Yamato *dotaku* or northern Kyushu bronze weaponry. The bronze requirements of those two areas were far greater than those of Kibi, even if we assume that the flat swords were made in the latter territory. Japanese archaeologists have tended to measure the importance of each area in the late Yayoi period by their independent imported raw material requirements and use. While the paucity of alternative data leaves few other sources, it could be that dangerous conclusions on the relative significance of various centres of population and culture have been drawn from this method of measurement.

The Mystery of the Tablets

In many of the late middle period Yayoi sites in Kibi, numerous small earthenware discs with two indentations in the sides have been discovered. These tablets, called *fundo*, measure up to 10 cm in diameter and 1 cm in thickness. They are very brittle, indicating quite high firing temperatures, and are decorated with small comb patterns and lines of small deep holes around the edges. In the San-in district, on the coast of Osaka bay, and in Yamaguchi prefecture, a few have also been found. So far about one hundred examples have been discovered, most of them in Kibi, while a few have been excavated in late Yayoi sites. Many of the *fundo* are missed during excavations for they are mostly broken owing to their brittle character and are easily mistaken for pot sherds. The comb patterns are composed of straight and oscillating lines, and the small edge holes are often partially outlined like eyebrows.

The initial temptation is to link the *fundo* with the shaman *dogu* ('figurines') and masks of the Jomon period, but this connection flounders on two objections. Firstly, no *fundo* have been found in early Yayoi period sites and, secondly, the shaman religion of the hunting people of the Jomon period was totally dissimilar from the superstitions of the settled rice growers of Yayoi.

The *Dotaku* Masks

Most academics agree that the *dotaku* were a Yamato-produced derivation of a Chinese bronze bell. In Kibi and other Inland Sea areas and in the San-in district a small number of *dotaku* have, however, been found which are quite different in size and decoration from Yamato *dotaku*; most of these have been found in Kibi at Ashimori and at Fukuda in Aki-gun, in Hiroshima prefecture. Unlike the Yamato *dotaku* the Kibi versions are much smaller and the decoration is in bands of both saw-tooth and fretwork patterns. On the upper part the eyes and eyebrows seen on the *fundo* can also be found, giving the impression of a stylized face somewhat similar to those often found on early Chinese bronzes. These Kibi *dotaku* could therefore be copies of mainland prototypes. There is no obvious connection between these *dotaku* and the *fundo* other than the appearance of similar decorations on both.

The use of the *dotaku* is still not clearly understood but their importance in Yayoi culture is undisputed. The resonant note that such objects might produce when struck could have transfixed simple agrarian people when first heard by them; the strange sounds, combined with the sun's reflections from their highly polished surfaces, may have been enough to produce fear in a people whose life revolved around superstitions concerning the sun and its influence on the all-important rice crop. The people who bore these instruments may have been considered agents of the sun with influence over its power and the ability to implement its demands.

The fact that the *fundo* are found to have similar decoration to that found on *dotaku* suggests to me that they were used as a kind of talisman. That the same decoration appears on the flat bronze swords, which were also possibly made in Kibi, further suggests the importance of both Yamato and northern Kyushu in their influence on Kibi and other Inland Sea areas. The swords, though not making such an impressive sound, would reflect the sun's rays; the addition of the common *dotaku* sawtooth and fretwork designs could have had great symbolism and may indicate the interrelationships between the three

kinds of objects to these simple, superstitious people.

The Magical Powers of the *Fundo*

The very few *dotaku* in existence and the distance between their incidence in Kibi and elsewhere suggest that, though rare, they played an important role in the lives of the people. It would have been impossible for individuals, or even families, to use such rare and sacred objects for their private purposes. It has been suggested that the *dotaku* with thin sawtooth decorated flanges around the edge were used as sundials; if they were placed in an east-west position, the shadow cast on the sawtooth marks might indicate the time. The ancients worked on an eleven hour day, the two casting holes at the top section, common to all *dotaku*, may have been used to determine midday. The connection between *dotaku* and agriculture in terms of the working day is obvious: to simple people, the *dotaku*'s position between the sun and themselves must have been one of sinister power and this could be an explanation of the respect in which they appear to have been held. Individuals may, on the other hand, have kept the *fundo* for personal use. The fact that many are found with almost identical decoration to that found on bronze *dotaku* suggests a belief that the power of the *dotaku* would enter the *fundo* if its decoration were similar.

In Kibi some *dotaku* were made of clay but

6. Clay *fundo* tablets believed to be magical talismans, third–fourth century AD. The *fundo* are unique to the Kibi culture although a few of them have been found in other areas of western Japan. The markings on them are similar to those found on the ceremonial flat bronze swords and bronze *dotaku*. They may have been given to their owners by shaman necromancers.

The Soja City Office.

these are much smaller and very rare and they appear to have been precise miniatures of the bronze originals. The connection between the clay *dotaku* and the *fundo* currently puzzles archaeologists. *Fundo* have been found at the same sites as the human-face bronze *dotaku* but no example has yet been discovered where clay *dotaku* are found together with bronze. This could indicate that the *fundo* had superior powers. They may have been a form of talisman guarding against evil spirits in humans and animals. The human face often drawn on the *fundo* takes both stylized and realistic forms. There is little doubt that a connection existed between the two objects but the apparent lower status of the clay *dotaku* is hard to explain.

In the later Yayoi period, Kibi people were probably not as advanced as those of other areas, who had contact with the Asian mainland, and fell under its influence. The appearance of the strange *fundo* and clay *dotaku* only in Kibi has led archaeologists to infer that the Kibi culture was introspective and that its artifacts evolved after their initial introduction without reference to external influences. Northern Kyushu was the gate to the Japanese archipelago while the Yamato people were culturally and socially the most advanced. Kibi lay between these two strong powers but even though it was probably weaker, it managed to preserve its identity and appears to have manufactured its own versions of ceremonial and religious paraphernalia.

Where was Toma?

The whereabouts of the Kingdom of Yamatai and its vassal kingdom Toma have been debated for centuries. Recently computers have been used to try and unravel the mystery, and novelists have whipped up public speculation and excitement, but a solution is nowhere to be found.

The Chinese gave, in the *Wei-Chih,* 'Chronicles of the Kingdom of Wei', written in the third century AD, both the distance and time a journey would take from China to Japan, but even so the location of Yamataikoku could be either in northern Kyushu or Yamato. In deciding which is correct the position of Toma is important. The *Wei-Chih* also tells us that there were 70,000 households in Yamataikoku, and 50,000 in Toma. As we have shown, the Inland Sea was, in ancient times, a vital trade route, so if the Yamato district was Yamataikoku then doubtless Toma would have been somewhere along the Inland Sea. The great Edo historian, Hakuseki Arai (1657–1725) believed that Toma was near Tomo in Bingo, western Kibi. Naturally he was basing his supposition on the similarity of name sounds which could be dangerously simplistic. Should his theory be viable, then it is equally reasonable to propose the Tama of Tamashima, a suburb of Kurashiki, or the Tama of Tamano City on the Kibi Inland Sea coast as equal contenders. His Kibi placement guess is probably correct, however, though for the wrong reasons.

Kibi in Late Yayoi

By the second and third centuries AD, Japan had entered what has been called the late Yayoi period. In Kibi, the three great rivers had formed rich delta regions which attracted settlements and over the years these villages had grown in size. For much of the earlier Yayoi period the paddy fields had changed little, but by the end of the Yayoi period advances in method and size were very rapid. At Tsushima the land area had increased with rich silt deposits. Irrigation canals were being built, and the Asahi River was being harnessed to flood the fields. The villages became larger still.

In the Tsushima district it is possible to study the gradual development of the paddy systems through the stratification of the soil. It is also possible to see that the soil was rich in iron and manganese. The irrigation canals show that the farmers had learnt to plant their rice on dry fields which they could then flood and drain at will—a similar system to that employed today. Such work would require a communal effort in larger villages; this in turn implies some form of authority and the emergence of a simple agrarian hierarchy. The headman was probably chosen with regard to religious status and his authority would have involved shamanistic and superstitious influences.

The rapid advances in paddy size and technology were due to the greater availability of iron—although very few iron implements of the period are found, suggesting that they were still precious objects. By the later Yayoi, stone tools seem to have become obsolete.

From the larger late Yayoi villages increasing amounts of pottery have been recovered. The styles of this pottery differ from region to region and researchers are currently at work collating the different characteristics of the pottery by area, thereby hoping to shed more light on the location of the kingdoms of Yamatai and Toma. In the early Yayoi period there was little evidence of a difference in pottery from one area to another. In the mid-Yayoi period in Kibi and other Inland Sea regions, examples of comb-scratched decoration have been found but larger caches of similar style excavated in Yamato suggest that Kibi and the other areas were influenced by that district. By the late Yayoi period, however, the pottery of the two had diverged in style and Kibi pottery was quite distinctive. At this time long-necked pots were being produced. These had rings around the neck and body and were slender in proportion to their height. Some wide-mouthed short-necked pots with strong bodies have also been found and it is clear that smaller vessels were placed on the top—these I would describe as stands. They have been found in various sizes and the style is now known as *Jotoshiki* after the Joto site in Kurashiki where they were first found. Pottery strongly influenced by the Joto style has been found in other regions, but the greatest number of villages producing this distinctive styled pottery were in Kibi. The potters' skills had developed to the point where they were using spatulas on the inside of their clay-coiled pots to produce thin earthenware.

This technique later spread from Kibi to other areas in Japan and is particularly evident in the later Hajiki and Sue wares of the Tumulus period. This is evidence that in the Yamatai period, Kibi was not merely a stopping place for Yamato-bound trading vessels but had its own culture and characteristics. It was a country in its own right and as similar as any other so far discovered to the Toma kingdom, vassal of the kingdom of Yamatai described by the Chinese historians.

7. A long-necked jar and stand excavated at Yakage, central Kibi, third century AD. The style of these magnificent early ceramics is unique to Kibi and point to a culture which was introverted and not so dependent on external authority. Jars and stands such as this are often painted in cinnabar which was thought to be an elixir of everlasting life. They were placed close to graves to hold offerings to the dead. Often the grave walls were also painted with cinnabar.

The Kurashiki City Office.

King or Emperor?

It should be noted that the term 'emperor' as used by the ancient Japanese histories is inaccurate and the Japanese term *tenno* translated as Emperor is misleading. The correct English definition of the rank should be at best king. I have used this term throughout except in passages where the word 'Emperor' helps the text in relation to the unification of the Wa branch states under a Yamato emperor.

The term 'emperor' as written in the first histories was applied deliberately to bolster national prestige and pride and to attempt to put the nation on the same level as that of a highly civilized China. Japan never had an empire or was in any sense akin to ancient Rome, China, or nineteenth century Britain. The use of such a term to describe a loose rule over a number of federated states is absurd.

The third century AD chronicles of the Chinese Wei dynasty describes the Wa states as numerous and ruled by priestesses or chieftains. The paramount ruler is named Himiko and is described as a crafty, calculating shaman priestess who ruled over a country called Yamataikoku—yet to be geographically identified. Himiko is also reputed to have unified many of the Wa states. Where she ruled and other details of her life have been lost in time. Perhaps, one day, archaeology will unearth the truth about her and her domain.

The compilers of Japan's first histories placed the first 'emperor' at 660 BC. He was given the posthumous title (in Chinese fashion) of Jimmu. The Chinese cyclical system was used in dating. One cycle was sixty years. The first historians soon found that they had too many years and not enough emperors or stories. Imagination came to the rescue and many impressive passages were lifted from Korean and Chinese writings. Names were given, changed and invented. The entire 'imperial' line up to the mid-fourth century is fictitious. Dangerous conclusions can be reached by underestimating this.

The author's task is to unravel some of the distortions of the early fabricators and attempt to correct these exaggerations wherever possible.

Perhaps the modern Japanese should cease using the term 'emperor' in English language references and apply the more apt title of 'king'. Until we finally refer to the ancient monarchs in proper terms, and examine their tombs for more evidence of the distortions of the eighth century visionaries, the easier it will be to understand this very complex period. With the removal of the symbols left to us through the early chronicles and the later nineteenth century bureaucrats, a start will have been made.

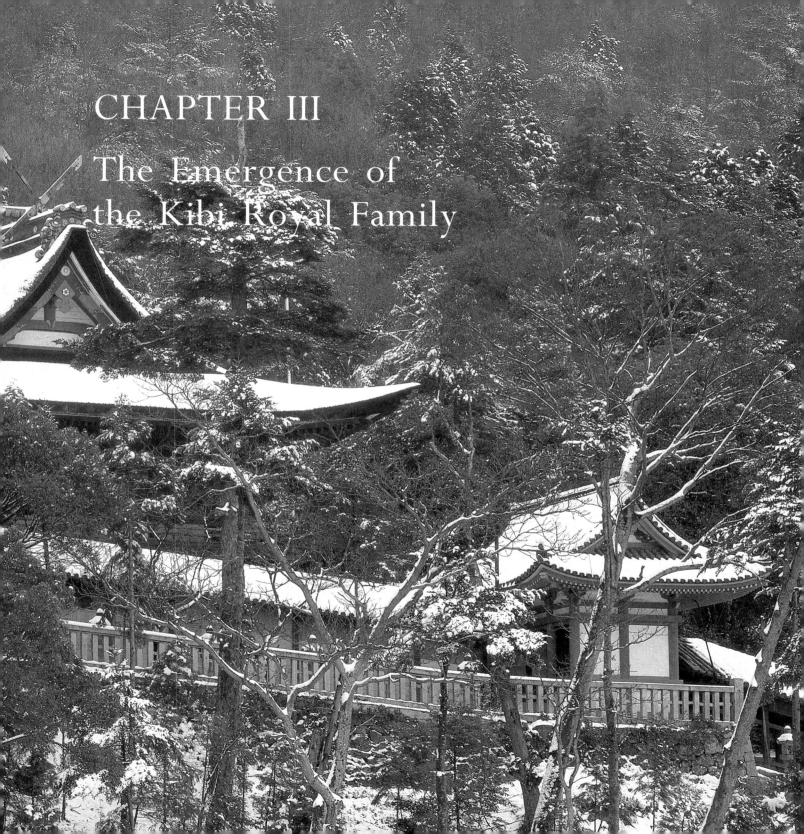

CHAPTER III
The Emergence of the Kibi Royal Family

The Tumulus Connection

About twenty years ago a strange hoop-like piece of fired pottery was discovered in a vegetable patch at Imoyama near Yakage in western Kibi. The Kurashiki Archaeological Museum, which examined the find, first thought it to be from a *haniwa* ('figurine') base or stand. The clay was very fragile but the firing temperatures seemed to correspond to those used for *haniwa*. Later, about 80 metres away from the hoop, a large stone coffin was discovered, followed by many more clay fragments which, archaeologists concluded, were mainly from *takatsuki* ('bowls with tall feet') and *tsubo* ('jars'). Then more hoops of clay came to light; the pottery dated from the late Yayoi period, about 100–150 years earlier than the stone coffin. At a subsequent survey of the Yakage site, some thirty closely-grouped graves were exposed. The pottery found nearby seemed to have been used as offerings to the cemetery rather than to the individual dead. The fragments were unlike any known outside Kibi and this pointed to the conclusion that the transition from the Yayoi culture to the new Tumulus age at Kibi was different from that experienced elsewhere.

Similar pottery has been found at Miyayama, Miwa and Iyobeyama near Soja City in central Kibi and at Tsushima in Okayama City. The pots presumably played a part in funerals or memorial services, and are believed to date from the period when the Tumulus culture first began in the Yamato. The form of the pottery looks like a later development of the *jotoshiki*-style jar on tall feet and of the long-necked jar.

We suspect that the Tumulus culture spread from the Yamato district in all directions, but the process of change in each area from the Yayoi culture to the new is a conundrum. If we could find the key we would no doubt find the answer to the whereabouts of the mysterious kingdoms of Yamataikoku and Toma.

In the central Kibi villages many late Yayoi earthenware stands have been discovered, each between 10 and 15 cm in diameter. Similar stands are also found in Yamato and elsewhere but those in Kibi are much more numerous and their decoration much superior. The stands were not for everyday use but were intended to be used as ceremonial stands for pots containing offerings of food for the spirits of the dead.

We know very little about how the religious festivals of the time were conducted. Each village would have had a chief priest or priestess who does not seem to have been segregated to a great extent from the rest of the village since there was no distinction at burial. The pottery found in and around the villages is a mixture of domestic and religious ceremonial. In Yamato separate wooden coffins were used but in Kyushu cyst-style *shiseki* or 'community graves' outlined with stones and accommodating several bodies are common. It is only in the late Yayoi period that ceremonial pottery appears.

About thirty years ago, in Kibi some group graves were uncovered but they are not outlined with stones to the same extent as in Kyushu. Usually the Kibi graves are simple trenches in the earth in which the dead were laid. Only very small personal objects such as beads or talismans were buried with them. The grave was filled with little ceremony and no markers were included, unlike in the later Tumulus period. Ceremonial pottery was placed above the grave. To begin with, there was apparently little distinction between the domestic and ceremonial pottery. Everyday bowls were used for offerings to the dead but as the practice grew in popularity a specific funeral ceramic offering evolved. This is evident from the numbers of *takatsuki* found in cemeteries, compared with domestic sites. The funerary vessels also began to be more highly decorated. Then stands with wide mouths and short feet were replaced by increasingly taller *takatsuki*. The bodies of the stands were incised with patterns which had existed in the Yayoi Period, placed in lines and occasionally separated by the clay hoops to strengthen the urns. These hoops are a later development of the hoops found at Yakage from the late Yayoi; on special vessels the hoops are sometimes decorated. Both the ceremonial stands and pots were beautifully painted with cinnabar (crystalized mercuric sulphide—vermilion).

The Story from the Graves

Ceremonial pottery was not presented to every grave but rather to clusters of graves, sometimes great, sometimes small in numbers; these clusters may have represented family groups. It is hard to say whether the pottery was dedicated at burials or at later occasions such as memorial festivals. At the Yakage site, where a cluster of thirty graves was found, they separated into three groups, at each of which the pottery found was a little different. Each group was buried deep on a ridge of a small hill. The ceremonial pottery found near the surface was in the position where it had been placed some 1,700 years before. Each pot had been painted with cinnabar which, in places, had trickled down the sides in such fashion as to suggest that some had been painted at the graveside. Holes had been deliberately made in the bottoms of the bowls and this could imply a protection from theft and that those alive were barred from using vessels intended for the dead. It might also be that the holes were thus placed so as to facilitate the unimpeded progress of the contents downwards through the soil for the ultimate nourishment of the dead. From these practices historians have deduced that funeral services were held for the dead and the vessels used were given a shallow covering above the graves. The belief was probably that the dead persons' faculties passed onto those who performed the ceremonies. In the case of a person with particular talents, he would be set apart both in life and in death, and attributed a degree of immortality. Although the grave would be much the same as those nearby, he or she clearly would have been a leader; this status was the first step towards that of a ruler in the modern sense.

Kibi and *Haniwa*

The unusual pottery fragments discussed earlier, which were found at Takage and later in other parts of Kibi near Soja and Okayama Cities, have also been unearthed as far east as Hyogo pre-

8. A *tokushu kidai* or special jar stand excavated at the Joto ruins near Kurashiki City. Late Yayoi period (c. AD 2OO). *Tokushu kidai* are virtually unique to the Kibi culture. The wonderful designs incised and cut out on the clay bodies are also found on bronzes and stone. These stands are believed to have been the forerunners of the *haniwa* figurines which were later used to decorate the circumference of the great tombs. Dishes of food would have been placed on these stands.

The Okayama Prefecture Museum.

fecture, near Fukuyama City in the west and north in Shimane prefecture. The centre of manufacture of this pottery and the area where fragments are most prolific is on the Kibi plain between Soja and Okayama cities. This area is known to have become the centre of power of the Kibi kingdom. At the time this pottery was manufactured, the people of the Yamato district had started to construct large tumuli above the ground. In Kibi, however, burial of the dead was carried out far from village settlements usually in cemeteries on the top of small hills. Pottery related in many ways to the later *haniwa* has been found at these cemetery sites. A common variety is the *tokushu-kidai* cylinder of some size upon which jars containing food offerings were placed; these cylinders are the forerunners of the cylindrical bases which were later used to support the pottery *haniwa* figurines placed around the top of tumuli. *Tokushu-kidai* cylinders are open at both ends and are of equal diameter along their length. They were partially buried for support and acted as stands; utilitarian jars were placed upon them. The shape of these cylindrical stands is very similar to the later *entohaniwa* or 'chimney *haniwa*', found in both Kibi and Yamato. They are painted in traditional designs which are still discernible, although the cinnabar used has faded.

In the Nara basin there is a keyhole-shaped tumulus believed to have been the grave of an early princess. It is called the Princess Totomomoso tumulus. One theory is that this tomb is that of the mysterious Himiko, queen of the Yamatai. In this tumulus and nearby, fragments of pottery clearly showing the influence of the Kibi *tokushu-kidai* cylinder have been found. This Yamato tumulus discovery is not unique; in nearby Kyoto prefecture at the Inari tumulus similar fragments were also found. All were examples of a later style of *tokushu-kidai* cylinder which had clearly developed the characteristics of early *haniwa*. From these finds I suspect that there is a strong relationship between the Kibi *tokushu-kidai* cylinders and the later tumulus culture of Yamato. In the overall picture of early Japanese history, an understanding of the beginnings of the Tumulus period is of great importance. Although we do not yet fully understand the relationship between Kibi and Yamato at this time, the evidence that such a relationship did exist is derived from the Kibi *tokushu-kidai* cylinders and their influence on later Yamato ceramics.

Graveyard of the Kings

When transitional ceramics of the Yayoi and Tumulus periods are discussed in relation to Kibi, reference is almost always made to the *tokushu-kidai* cylinders and the offertory jars they supported. These ceramic forms are the earliest accepted examples known to date from the beginning of the Tumulus period. When construction of the new Sanyo Shinkansen railway was at its peak, a further exciting discovery was made.

At the north-west of Kurashiki, close to a very late Yayoi cemetery which was completely destroyed by a new housing development, is a low hill called Obosan ('King Cemetery Hill') on the summit of which eighty small tumuli were dis-

9. A later development of the *tokushu kidai* stand with storehouse on the top. Excavated at Obosan (King's cemetary), third-fourth century AD. It is interesting to note that the early term for emperor in ancient Japanese was Takakura, 'raised storehouse'. The symbolism is obvious. A reference in the first King Jimmu (665 BC) section of the *Nihoshoki* refers to the construction of a palace 'raised on one pillar' in Buzen (modern Yamaguchi prefecture) before the king arrived in Kibi from Kyushu on his 'eastern conquests'. With appropriate 60 year cycle adjustments, the dates for this stand and the reference to the raised palace almost coincide in time and place. Could this clay model represent this palace and further prove that Obosan was indeed the gravesite of the first Puyo/Kayan conqueror – alias Jimmu? This model is the forerunner of the later *haniwa* figurines which suggests that the Kibi culture influenced other areas in eastern Japan very strongly. It seems certain that because the area near Obosan was the landing place of the conquerors, the communities in the vicinity were well garrisoned, sophisticated and put up some resistance to the invaders before the defeat.

The Kurashiki Archaelogical Museum.

covered. Obosan is a quiet, pine covered feature lying to the south of what seems to have been the power center and most important part of ancient Kibi. Through the pine trees and low valleys to the north-east can be seen the enormous keyhole-shaped Tsukuriyama tumulus—the largest in Kibi and fourth largest in Japan. To the east are the Hihata-akai Temple ruins from the Hakuho period (AD 645–710), where tiles have been excavated, while to the north is the Yabe Temple from the Tempyo period (AD 710-794). Also nearby at Hoita, and now completely destroyed, where the Shinkansen railway enters a tunnel, was a kiln site where the tiles for these two temples were manufactured. On a plateau on the summit of Obosan are two mysterious rocks. They are known as *myoto-iwa* ('husband and wife') rocks; nearby is the late Yayoi graveyard. About thirty years ago, when the area seemed to be in imminent danger of destruction from the construction of the new housing complex, a careful archaeological survey was conducted. It was decided that the rocks had no connection with the cemetery. But during the survey another tumulus was discovered to the west of the rocks and nearby was a hole in which wooden remains, probably of a coffin, seemed to have been buried. A further ten graves were found in a group while to one side of the group was a deep trench in which stones and pottery were found.

In general, tumuli of this period contain *tokushu-kidai* cylinders, but this example revealed only jars. Later in the survey a cylinder was found close by, but it is different from any other yet found. The diameter of the base is greater than that of the mouth and the middle section is reinforced by three hoops. On the top is a fine clay model of a building. It is so far the only specimen of its type and age found in Japan.

Previously it had generally been thought that the *tokushu-kidai* cylinders had been used since the end of the Yayoi period purely as stands for the presentation of offerings to the dead. Many archaeologists now believe that the cylinders have a special significance rather than being mere stands. The Obosan discovery of a cylinder with a model house upon it may have clarified their real purpose and removed some areas of doubt and misunderstanding that had existed previously.

The Palace of the Gods

From excavations throughout Kibi and elsewhere in Japan, we are familiar with the design of dwellings in the later Yayoi period; a wide shallow hole was dug and wooden pillars were placed in the middle of the hole to support a sloping roof of grass and reeds. This basic style of domestic architecture was used since Jomon times a thousand years or more before and had hardly changed. During the Yayoi period, special stilt-supported store-houses were constructed, with functional accessories such as ventilation windows and doors. Evidence of the existence of these buildings is found in the decoration on a ceremonial bronze *dotaku*. The famous Ohashi *dotaku*, which was discovered in Kagawa prefecture across the Inland Sea from Kibi, clearly depicted a store-house with a ladder, and a jar discovered at the Toko site near Nara had a similar drawing on it. No other examples are known.

For about a century after the construction of the tumuli on Obosan, pictures of buildings were used as decoration on various objects. A large bronze mirror found near Nara has four interesting decorations of houses moulded on the back. One is a typically Yayoi pit-dwelling, another a raised store-house and the others single and double-storeyed buildings. These four different buildings probably represent the sum of the architecture of the time. At another tumulus site near Nara, two bronze swords with pommels in the form of buildings have been excavated. One of these swords has a Chinese late Han dynasty (second century AD) date inlaid in gold upon the blade. The sword blades seem to be of Chinese manufacture and the pommels a later Japanese addition. The house-shaped pommels are very similar to one of the buildings depicted on the bronze mirror. Given that the bronze swords and the mirror were found in tumuli close to each other and that the craftsmanship and metal used are similar, some scholars believe they originated from the same workshop, possibly even from the hand of the same craftsman. Even if the mirror and the pommels were made some time before they were buried, when compared with other mirrors they are some decades later than the clay model building found on Obosan. The latter is a product of the Kibi culture, the others from the Yamato. The Obosan clay model building predates the later Yamato house *haniwa* by about one hundred years. It is central to the study of the architecture of the early Tumulus period, the transition of the *tokushu-kidai* cylinders to

haniwa, from simple festivals to elaborate rituals and from priests speaking on behalf of spirits to the emergence of rulers.

The *tokushu-kidai* cylinders had abstract decorations painted on them in cinnabar; the Obosan find had no decoration other than the model building. Many questions arise when the *tokushu-kidai* cylinders and the Obosan model are compared.

Academic interest in the death customs of this period and the associated funerals and festivals is increasing. There is a suggestion that they varied from clan to clan in Kibi. It could be that the clan living near Obosan was more advanced than others and that the wooden building (as depicted in the clay model) within the community may indicate the emergence of a class system. The clay model may have represented a house for the spirits; in advanced communities where special raised floor store-houses were constructed, a house for the gods may also have been provided. It is interesting to note that the ancient Japanese term for emperor was *takakura* ('raised store house'). At this transitional time (c. AD 200) the Chinese historians began to mention the mysterious Japanese Queen Himiko of Yamataikoku. Times were turbulent, and remained so after Himiko's death. The picture certainly becomes slightly clearer in the light of recent archaeological findings. From the Chinese chronicles, scholars are now inclined to believe that the burial sites where the *tokushu-kidai* cylinders and jars were found are the resting places of priests and priestesses or patriarchs—the leaders of the various Kibi clans. Gradually, the clans united under a central authority from which an overall ruler was chosen, until eventually one clan achieved such dominance that it became a royal family. The Obosan site is, in all probability, the cemetery of the first really powerful Kibi royal family; its proximity to the enormous tumuli and religious buildings of great significance of later times might support this theory.

I have so far devoted much space to the archaeological work that has taken place in Kibi over the past thirty years. Although the finds are many and the resultant conclusions few, an overall picture does begin to appear and a clearer understanding of ancient Kibi and its importance in the early centuries AD has become possible. By the year AD 200, Kibi had reached a stage whereby a ruling class had appeared and the clans had begun to merge into a tribe. In my opinion, one of the strongest pieces of evidence of a developing class system is the gradual appearance of larger and larger tombs and the numerous artifacts, presumably personal possessions, found in them. Only the existence of a ruling class could justify such particular effort.

A sophisticated China had been making cultural and political inroads into Korea since the last centuries BC. The iron culture was introduced to Korea from the north by Chinese refugee groups. This culture rapidly replaced that of bronze; the refugees established themselves in groups and quite rapidly the iron–bronze culture, with strong Chinese influence, spread southward to Japan, ultimately reaching Kibi via Kyushu. The pit dwellings in which the early inhabitants lived were gradually replaced by wooden houses which the new iron tools made comparatively easy to build.

These early Korean-influenced Kibi people were undoubtedly animists. They believed that natural phenomena and forces were controlled by spirits which also controlled human lives and fortunes. The rivers, rocks, trees and mountains of ancient Kibi all harboured spirits. The most powerful spirit was the sun, which was naturally all important to a society dependent on agriculture. It is particularly significant that the late Yayoi graveyards were positioned on the tops of hills, nearest to villages, to be as close to the sun as possible. Kibi animism gradually developed under Korean influence into shamanism, where particular people, generally women, were thought to have special contact with, or powers over, these spirits.

The clans of Kibi were probably exogamous, prohibiting marriage within the clan; this would have caused much strife between rival clans and ultimately led to the formation of a tribal society. The development of the tribes of Kibi appears to have owed much to refugees from more developed areas such as Korea and China. This suggestion is supported by local folklore and legend. One such legend concerns the Mountain Demon, called the Ura, who was believed to be Korean.

From the numerous excavations in Kibi it is reasonable to assume that by the end of the third century and beginning of the fourth, in some areas, the ruling class lived in quite elaborate wooden houses and, like the Koreans, probably dressed in silk, wore leather shoes and personal jewelry such as necklaces, earrings and wrist bells; they carried ornate imported swords and decorated in local style and they kept slaves who

10. The great Kibitsu Shrine. The buildings date from the fourteenth–fifteenth century AD; however, shrines would have been present at this spot for a thousand years before the current construction. This complex is dedicated to the spirit of Kibitsu Hiko's military exploits. There is an archery pavilion within the precincts. This shrine is the most important Shinto edifice in Kibi. Nearby is a smaller but equally lovely shrine dedicated to Kibitsu Hiko's spirit. His tomb is believed to be on the top of the hill on the sides of which these buildings are found. The main shrine sits on a white plastered base symbolizing water and ancient Kibi's power over the seaways close by.

34

had been taken as prisoners of war. Commoners lived in the old pit dwellings and dressed in hemp and straw.

The Chinese chronicles record that the people sang, drank and danced at festivals of the spirits connected with agriculture, which was their livelihood. The appearance of more and more grave ware in third and fourth century burials suggests the beginnings of a belief in the afterlife.

Prince Kibitsu-Hiko

There is little academic dispute with the theory that most of the tumulus culture spread outwards from Yamato in all directions. Simultaneously, the tribal groups in outlying areas were gradually coming under the Yamato power and joining the Yamato league. The country was slowly becoming unified. The two hundred year period between the beginning of the fourth century AD, and the end of the fifth, was very turbulent. This is clear both from the Chinese histories of the time and from modern archaeological research. The leading families and clans no doubt fought among themselves and, in Yamato, the royal family often changed. Even in the *Kojiki* of AD 712 and the *Nihonshoki* of AD 720, in which the 'emperor' was regarded as a god, his ancestors are said to have fought against each other to achieve power. It is interesting that although the authors of the histories, under imperial instruction, were expected to edit out all unfavourable references and keep only the good, they nevertheless refer to lengthy disputes and squabbles in the chap-

ters on the 'Age of the Gods'. These accounts must relate to these violent two centuries in Yamato. Similar unrest doubtless occurred in other districts including Kibi.

The best known but most complex Kibi personage to appear in the two early histories is Kibitsu-Hiko, one of four generals who, under royal decree, was sent westward to pacify the provinces. His spirit is enshrined at the beautiful Kibitsu Shrine built on the outskirts of central Kibi near Okayama City in the Muromachi period (1392–1573). Strangely, we know little about him other than these references in the early histories.

According to the *Nihonshoki*, Kibitsu-Hiko was the son of the 'Emperor' Korei, who reigned 290–215 BC and who lived 128 years. During the reign of the 'Emperor' Sujin (reigned 97–30 BC) he was one of the four generals who were sent to the west. His younger brother, Waka-Take-Hiko is on record as the ancestor of the Omititled families of Kibi, and later served with the great General Yamato-Takeru-no-Mikoto in the conquest of Etsu-Mino. One of Waka-Take-Hiko's daughters married Yamato-Takeru-no-Mikoto. In the Kojiki, a different account appears. Kibitsu-Hiko is again described as the son of the 'Emperor' Korei but is said to have been sent by his father with Waka-Hiko-Take-Kibitsu-Hiko to Kibi. The Kojiki does not refer to the four generals during the reign of Sujin, but instead tells of two princes who were sent to Tamba and Etsu.

In both the *Nihonshoki* and the *Kojiki* the wife of the 'Emperor' Keiko (reigned AD 71–130), Harima-no-Inabi-no-oho-Iratsume, is described. In the *Kojiki* she is said to be the daughter of

Waka-Take-Kibitsu-Hiko but in the *Nihonshoki* her parentage is not recorded. Curiously, the *Nihonshoki* states that the daughter of Waka-Take-Hiko married Yamato-Takeru-no-Mikoto but the *Kojiki* does not. Also in the *Kojiki* is a statement that the general who went east with Yamato-Takeru-no-Mikoto was the ancestor of the Omi of Kibi but his name was not Waka-Take whose sister Okibi-Take-Hime was one of the wives of Yamato-Takeru-no-Mikoto. The complications and confusion are obvious, and although the histories were written only eight years apart, the stories concerning Kibitsu-Hiko and his family are totally inconsistent. From these accounts of the eastern and western conquests of the princes or generals we can, however, see the way in which the later Yamato court of the eighth century favoured the gradual merging of the tribes into leagues. It is similarly certain that Kibitsu-Hiko was an important person; whether he was from Yamato, from Kibi or even Korea is not clear.

The Asahi River runs through the central part of Okayama City. The delta which this river created has been an important dwelling area since the Yayoi period—nearby are some of the most important and notable tumuli in Kibi. From the east of the Asahi River on Tatsunokuchi Hill, the Okayama plain can be seen. A tumulus was discovered on this hill, about thirty years ago. It is called Bizen Kurumazuka and was found by unauthorized diggers. Thirteen Chinese bronze mirrors were excavated; fortunately, these were discovered and confiscated by the authorities. This discovery was of great importance and significance in the study of the early Tumulus period.

At about the same time, Professor Yukio Kobayashi of Kyoto University, a leading authority on bronze mirrors, discovered a cache of more than thirty-six bronze mirrors, of which thirty-two were from several similar moulds, in a tumulus near Kyoto. They were decorated with Chinese gods and animals. To the astonishment of scholars of Kibi, some of the thirteen mirrors found in the Bizen Kurumazuka tumulus were from the same moulds as some of the thirty-two discovered by Professor Kobayashi.

It is recorded in the Chinese Wei-Chih (AD 212) that a presentation from the Wei emperor of numerous bronze mirrors was made to Queen Himiko's (Yamataikoku) ambassador in an exchange of gifts. Professor Kobayashi is of the opinion that some of the mirrors could be part of the Wei presentation. The dating of the mirrors is compatible with his theory. Kobayashi also believes that the influence of the various areas or regions can be measured by the number of mirrors found, similar to the Kyoto find. This 'mirror distribution' suggests that mirrors were imported from the mainland in very large quantities and then distributed to the rulers or patriarchs in numbers corresponding to the importance of each region. In the Bizen-Kurumazuka tumulus, four mirrors were found which were from the same moulds as some in the Kyoto cache. In one case there were even two examples from a single mould.

The style of the mirrors found at Bizen-Kurumazuka has a stronger similarity with groups of mirrors found east of Yamato. As we are told in the early histories, Kibi-Take-Waka-Hiko the younger brother of Kibitsu-Hiko, went east with

11. The reverse side of a bronze mirror with moulded Chinese inscription and human figures; third century AD. Such mirrors have their origins in ancient China. Gifts of mirrors to Korean and Japanese rulers are recorded in the early Chinese histories. They were a status symbol and their ability to reflect the sun's rays is significant. The sun was the principal spirit within Shintoism. The mirror is one of the three Japanese imperial regalia, together with the sword and the *magatama* or comma-shaped bead, which symbolises a bear's claw and the power, strength and cunning of animals. The first mirrors would have entered Kibi from Korea.
The National Museum, Tokyo.

37

Yamato-Takeru to conquer Etsu and Mino. The timing of these eastern expeditions coincides neatly with the dates of the Wei Emperor's gifts of mirrors. It is therefore not unreasonable to suppose that the occupant of the Bizen-Kurumazuka tumulus had a very strong connection with the Yamato tribal league and may even have been one of the conquerors of the east. If this is the case, then the statements in the early histories that Kibi-Take-Waka-Hiko was the ancestor of the Omi of Kibi could be correct. The Bizen-Kurumazuka tumulus might then be the grave of either Kibitsu-Hiko or his younger brother Kibi-Take-Waka-Hiko. In any case the occupant must certainly have had some connection with the areas east of Yamato where the same patterns of mirrors are found.

North of Okayama, on Handayama Hill, near the Tsushima Yayoi period sites discussed in Chapter II, is a slope called Totsuki on which are two interesting tumuli excavated by the Okayama University Department of Archaeology. One of the tumuli was shaped in the classic *zempo koho fun* ('key-hole') style; the other is a narrow rectangular chamber with the sides and bottom lined with stones and rocks. These tumuli were named Totsuki '1' and '2', and from the former a very sophisticated *tokushu-kidai* cylinder was recovered. This is a later development of the cylinders discovered at Takage and Obosan and is an *ento* ('chimney shaped') *haniwa*. A jar-shaped *haniwa* without a bottom resembling one found at the Chausuyama tumulus near Nara, dating from the late fourth century, was also discovered. Totsuki '1' incorporated a stone-lined burial chamber but was not as rich in artifacts as the Bizen-Kurumazuka tumulus. Totsuki '2' was surrounded by twenty simple graves. No artifacts were recovered from it but in one of the surrounding burials a solitary string of beads was found. In the soil close to the surface was some late Yayoi pottery. The overall style of the Totsuki '2' tumulus is quite different from other early earth-mound tumuli.

If we simply compare the artifacts found in Kurumazuka and Totsuki '1' and '2', it seems clear that the person buried in Kurumazuka was more influential than the occupants of Totsuki '1' and '2'. The dating of the three tumuli is very close and the occupants of the tombs could even have known each other since the distance between the Totsuki tumuli and Kurumazuka is only one kilometre, in a straight line across the Asahi River. The distinction between respective occupants must have been determined by wealth and social status, and the size of the clan they led. Clearly, the grave at Kurumazuka had very strong ties with Yamato, while those at Totsuki did not. It seems possible that the Kurumazuka links with Kibi were not as strong as those of Totsuki, since the villages excavated to the south of Kurumazuka are much smaller than the communities to the south of Totsuki, where the major Yayoi period Tsushima settlement was found. By the beginning of the Tumulus period however, the settlements near Handayama had become significantly bigger than those to the south by Kurumazuka.

Korea at that time

Korea had a very colourful history in those distant times. The close proximity with China influenced it greatly.

The bronze culture, however, came into Korea from the north. This was not from China but through Scythian-Siberian influence. Bronze had been well known within these cultures long before 1000 BC.

As bronze usage developed a curious reaction appears in relation to ceramics on the peninsula and Japan. The old cord- or rope-marked styles were replaced by plainer ceramics suggesting that a different culture was responsible. At about the sixth or seventh century BC rice had been introduced from China which gradually stabilized the unsettled wandering characteristics of the society that previously existed. The clans or families began to group together into regional tribes and consequently a ruling class arose which was hitherto rare in Korea.

The eastern and southern clans continued in the old tradition and naturally this would have been the case on the Japanese archipelago. They were late starters. The predominant northern tribe was that of the Koguryo; however, above them in the Sungari river basins of Manchuria, were the Puyo people who later gave their name to the capital of the south-western kingdom of Paekche, after they had settled in that territory in the third century AD.

Huge dolmens then began to appear, heralding the presence of a strong ruling class. This practice spread south and across to Japan. Usually the dolmens consist of massive boulders laid out in a rectangular configuration with a large hewn stone slab laid on the top. In Korea the dolmen style differs between the north and the south. The northern Puyo styles are of greater height and are striking in appearance when compared with the smaller dolmens of the south. Curiously the taller style is found in Kibi but gradually became smaller as the Yayoi period developed.

The construction of such edifices would have been labour-intensive and commanded the energy of thousands of people. Only a slave-owning society such as the Puyo would have been in a position to direct such forces for the required periods of time. This labour was later directed to the construction of huge personal tombs which indicates evidence of a ruling class in both Korea and Japan. Manchurian influences are also evident in both countries, in the stone box tomb style burials which contained bronze artifacts in Scythian taste. Kibi is rich in these as the later fourth century AD Sakakiyama tumulus finds exemplify.

Enormous dolmens, the movement of rocks into shapes and patterns of geomantic design suggests the emergence of larger and larger political units—the pattern for which arrived on the archipelago some centuries after their introduction to the peninsula.

Free standing monoliths are also found throughout Korea. In Kibi they also exist in combination, in some cases, with a flatter stone which together are called *myoto-iwa* or husband and wife stones. These free stones are often phallic and are shaman interpretations of this subject which affects the lives of both humans and animals.

12. Front view of the Great Kibitsu Shrine.

Two Views of Prince Kibitsu-Hiko

On comparing the Totsuki tumuli and Kurumazuka, I am driven to speculate on who Kibitsu-Hiko really was and from where he came. To me, the most puzzling factor is that he is described in both the *Kojiki* and *Nihonshoki* as being of imperial blood and the son of the seventh Emperor Korei. Neither this emperor, however, nor those immediately before or for some time after him have been clearly identified and there is no reliable written or archaeological evidence that they existed.

But Kibitsu-Hiko must at one time have been the ruler of Kibi. Perhaps, after the formation of the Yamato state, his deeds and accomplishments were chronicled by the court historians as the acts of several different characters. He may have been an emissary of the Yamato court and its proconsul, or else ruler of Kibi in his own right. In either case, Kibi was a place of great importance. The transition of pottery cylinders into *haniwa* and the receipt of so many Chinese bronze mirrors would tend to support the theory that it was of central significance to the Yamato leagues in the early Tumulus period, when the power in Kibi may have been divided between two major clans, as the Totsuki and Kurumazuka discoveries imply.

The *Kojiki* and *Nihonshoki* describe, 400 years after the event, the story of the western conquests of Kibitsu-Hiko and Waka-Take-Hiko. To me it is quite clear that Kibi, in the third century, must have rivalled Yamato and had already developed a tribal league and royal family of its own. There are shrines to the memory of Kibitsu-Hiko at Bizen-Ichinomiya, Bitchu-Ichinomiya and Bingo-Ichinomiya, which means that his influence held sway throughout Kibi. As the Yamato state grew to power in the sixth and seventh centuries it could have dispatched military expeditions like those described in the *Kojiki* and *Nihonshoki*. At the dates implied by the two histories this seems unlikely, in spite of the efforts of later 'imperial' chroniclers to propound the contrary. My view is that the more the Yamato tribes tried to encroach on Kibi territory, the stronger Kibi tribal bonds became. I believe that this Kibitsu-Hiko was a general who repulsed the constant invasions of his territory and the great shrines dedicated to his memory, all over Kibi, are my witnesses.

The eighth century historians took Kibitsu-Hiko's admired life and deeds for their own purposes and made an artificial Yamato hero of him. There are other examples of this; in both works large sections of Chinese imperial history were lifted and interposed in the first Japanese histories to dress them up to be as impressive as those of China and Korea.

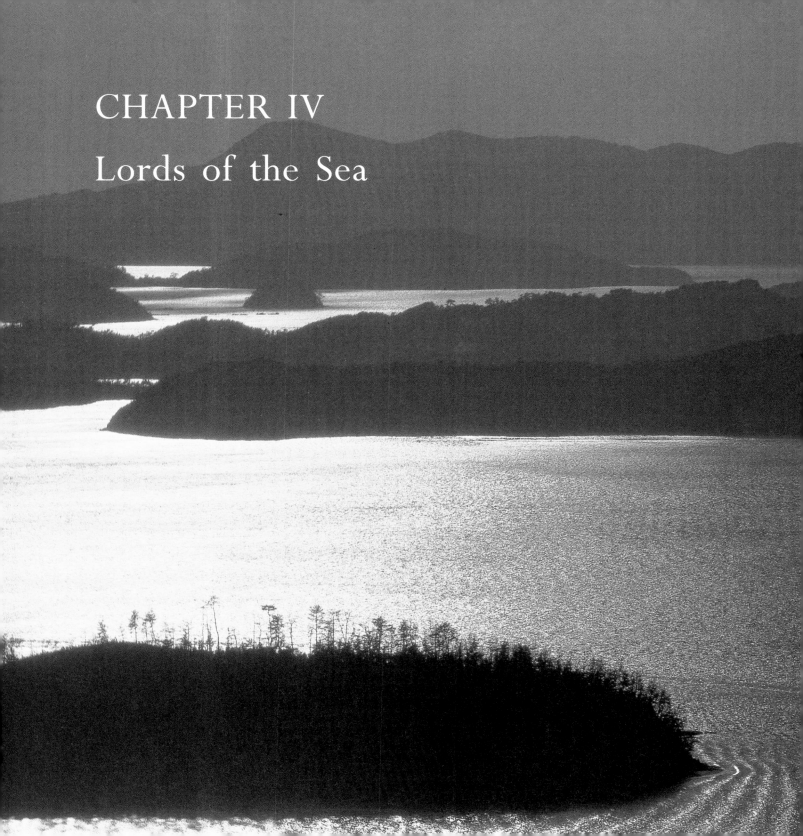

CHAPTER IV
Lords of the Sea

On the top of Mt Naka in the eastern hills of central Kibi is a tumulus which is also said to be the grave of Kibitsu-Hiko. In the classic keyhole shape and 150 metres in length, it is officially called the Nakayama Chausuyama tumulus. On the side of Mt. Naka, on which the tumulus was built, can be found the greatest shrine in Kibi and one of the finest in the country, called Kibitsu Jinja, first built in veneration of the heroic spirit of Kibitsu-Hiko, but the present buildings date only from the Muromachi period (1392–1573).

The front of Kibitsu Shrine faces the old *sanyo-do* (road), which led from Yamato into the western provinces and in Kibi crossed the Bizen delta and Soja plain. The *sanyo-do* is flanked by hills to the south and north and the shrine and tumulus are grouped at the narrowest and southernmost point. To the west of Mt Naka flows the Ashimori River; many Yayoi period ruins have been found along its banks. An ancient document, the *Dai-Anji-Kyu-Kishi*, says that, even into the Nara period, *ashi* reeds grew in abundance on both the east and west banks – a factor the Yayoi folk considered vital for good natural paddy land. The plain to the south of Mt Naka, which today is rich paddy, was at that time under the sea. The rounded front of the Nakayama Chausuyama tumulus faced the sea. This and its size are two reasons why it may be the last resting place of Prince Kibitsu-Hiko. Along the Inland Sea, there are many tumuli facing the sea, but it is in Kibi that they are most numerous. All the sea-facing tumuli are large and more than likely the graves of the great. The Kibi royal family, as we will see, was a powerful force at sea.

The most easterly tumuli in Kibi are a group of five at the tip of the Ushimado Peninsula facing Ushimado Bay. This peninsula protrudes into Okayama City. The tumuli are scattered on hillocks and are all of the classic keyhole shape, ranging in length from 50 to 90 metres. In all cases they are constructed from large rocks piled one on top of the other, in terraces, and in some cases the tumuli were moated. Perhaps the most unusual of the Ushimado group is the Kuroshima Tumulus in the centre of Kozima Island (not to be confused with Kojima). The tomb takes up almost the entire island, which faces Ushimado. At this tomb site, as at the others in the group, chimney-shaped *haniwa* were discovered; only at the Kuroshima tumulus were *keisho* ('figurine') *haniwa* found.

The Ushimado tumuli are the closest to the sea in Kibi. Tracing the ancient coastline from Ushimado in eastern Kibi to Matsunaga Bay in the west, we find a number of groups of tumuli, all apparently facing the sea and so positioned that sea traffic between Yamato, Kyushu and Korea could not miss sighting them. They are witnesses to the power of the region and their very size must have instilled fear and respect for the spirits of those whose tombs they were. The largest concentration of tumuli in Kibi is to be found on the hills of Misaoyama to the east of Okayama. One of these, the Minato Chausuyama Tumulus, is on a hilltop overlooking Kojima Bay, close to the mouth of the Asahi River. From this hilltop, one can discern the progressive stages of the natural reclamation of land towards Kojima Island. The Minato Chausuyama tumulus is 150 metres long, keyhole-shaped, and *haniwa* were buried around it.

Following the old coastline around the Bay of Kibi facing the great Kojima Island, we encounter numerous tumuli built on strategic hilltops commanding the sea lanes and major estuaries. About six kilometres west of the Misaoyama Hills is Mt Naka, on top of which is the Nakayama Chausuyama tumulus, designated by the Imperial Household Agency as the tomb of Prince Kibitsu-Hiko. Nearby is a fairly large keyhole-shaped tomb, 140 metres long, known as the Kuramayama tumulus. Although the front is untypically narrow, the shape is classic, with three terraces at the sides. Sherds of *ento* ('chimney-shaped') *haniwa* were found here, suggesting that the whole circumference of the top terrace at the rounded end had been studded with them. To the west of the Kuramayama tumulus is another very small, 30 metre-long, keyhole tomb; although unimportant in size, it commands a fine view of the sea. Further round the Bay of Kibi, across the Takahashi River at Yashima, west of present day Kurashiki City can be found part of a tumulus known as Tenozan. The square front, which faced the sea, has been destroyed, but the rear rounded section remains, and there *ento haniwa* were again found. From the remains, we can estimate its length at about 50 metres.

Moving further westward around the bay, tumuli become rarer. Obviously, with no large rivers and only small streams, rice was difficult to grow and the population dwindled. Matsunaga Bay to the north of the Hiuchi Nada Straits marks the western boundary of Kibi. Although the population here was probably small, a number of large tumuli have been found. The area is dotted with small islands which afforded ideal shelter for shipping. On the westernmost hill in Matsunaga Bay, on the inland side, were two keyhole tumuli, but these tombs were destroyed by construction work. They were probably between 50 and 70 metres long. The only complete tumulus extant on this boundary of Kibi is the Matsumoto tomb, which is square and is the largest in western Kibi; all these western tumuli offered fine views of the seaways and were largely constructed in the fifth century.

Tombs by the Sea

There is an interesting account, in the *Nihon-shoki*, concerning the return journey of Prince Yamato-Takeru to Yamato from a successful expedition against the Kumaso barbarians of central Kyushu. While sailing through the Bay of Kibi he encountered a 'malignant deity' who, with mischievous intent, sent forth a poisonous vapour by which the travellers were plagued. The Bay of Kibi 'formed a centre of calamity, therefore he slew the evil deity, the god of the ferry of this Bay of Kibi'. He reported to his father, the Emperor Keiko (AD 12–AD 130) how he had killed all the evil deities and threw open the ways by land and water alike. This account I find rather curious, for although it is undoubtedly fictitious, the fact that it was written in AD 720 gives us a clear idea of how the kings of Kibi and the area were then regarded by Yamato. The Bay of Kibi, central to trade with Kyushu and Korea, was without a doubt a running sore to the Yamato kings of the sixth and seventh cen-

Korea at that time

We have now reached the most complex and difficult period to understand in the early history of both countries: the missing fourth century AD. It is missing because no one appears able to sort it out correctly. Both modern Japanese and Korean historians allow the overtones of nationalism to cloud any sensible conclusions.

After the tribal communities formed themselves into leagues, kingdoms emerged. Korea, with its proximity to China, developed socially and culturally faster than Japan. The northern kingdom of Koguryo was the closest and through its complicated relationships to the north and to the west with China became a very sophisticated state—forming a government and society which earned the respect of China and envy elsewhere. Internal strife in China eventually put the two nations on a collision course. Border skirmishes developed into full scale war as the transition of one dynasty to another in China exacerbated the situation. These were tumultuous times in China as the once powerful borders fragmented. Koguryo was not slow in taking advantage of this weakness and soon attacked the Chinese border posts and drove the Chinese out of the territory China had occupied and held for the past four hundred years.

Paekche, the kingdom to the south-west of Koguryo, had been founded by the Manchurian Puyo tribes as they swept down the west coast of Korea together with their horses and slaves, ultimately dominating all the Kaya tribes to the south. Paekche came into being at about the same time that Koguryo expelled the Chinese. The two kingdoms then faced each other across a common border—the result was war, but not before Paekche had succeeded in unifying the tribes to the south. During the war the king of Koguryo was killed and Paekche was able to extend its territory further north and developed direct trade relations with China. To the south the Kayan/Puyo people had crossed to Japan and commercial relations were established with Kibi and the more populous Yamato basin to the east. Fierce resistance to the newcomers resulted in constant internecine fighting.

In eastern Korea, the kingdom of Silla was founded in the mid-fourth century. Silla's relationships with China were blocked by the kingdoms of Paekche and Koguryo. It did have relations with Japan probably with the Izumo tribes on the Japanese sea coast. Silla later formed an alliance with Koguryo which sent an army to assist Silla in repelling an attack from Japan.

Silla was a very different state to the other kingdoms. It was introspective and developed a culture of its own not reliant on China. Silla's role within Japanese historical development is extremely difficult to understand. That Silla was an agent-provocateur is well accepted. The histories of Japan and Korea vie with one another in presenting their causes, complaints and superiority. Silla was the wild card and the Japanese histories of the eighth century AD, as written, are particularly sensitive to the kingdom and seem to overplay its early importance. This could well be due to the fact that a new unified Silla had emerged by the eighth century. It was powerful, sophisticated and, unlike its predecessor of the fourth century, totally in control of its diplomacy, culture and economic relations. In short, the later Silla worried Japan. This is well reflected in the way the Japanese have chosen to deal with this close neighbour. A fear of Silla has caused obfuscation, distortion, and resulted in scholarly confusion whenever Silla is recorded or alluded to.

Much time can be wasted and wrong conclusions reached by overestimating these chauvinistic idiosyncrasies. The Paekche kingdom of western Korea was clearly the most influential with fourth and fifth century Japan. Archaeology proves this as do the later records, if interpreted correctly.

turies. Throughout the early parts of both the early histories we read only of victories, never defeats. Kibi is scarcely mentioned save for the occasional intermarriage. The Yamato kings treated their failures as the work of devils and vermin and Kibi attracted such descriptions in both the early histories.

The first tumuli were constructed close to the communities where the clan leaders lived and ruled. In early Kibi, the power of the leader came from success in agriculture and the tombs of dead leaders served to remind all people of their influences even after death.

Coastal Kibi differs from this pattern. I have described earlier how numerous large tombs were constructed from Ushimado in the east along the bay to Matsunaga in the far west. Ushimado, until Edo times, was constantly mentioned as a very important port for traffic through the Inland Sea. The hills bearing the Misaoyama group of tumuli drop steeply to the sea and behind them are larger hills separating Misaoyama from the Oku plain. The position of the tumuli and the existence of earlier shell mounds (indicating Jomon and Yayoi burials) at the foot of the hills shows where the sea then reached – for the Jomon people buried their dead as close to the sea as possible. This suggests that these tombs are the graves of the rulers of the important southeast sea entrance to Kibi. The tumuli extending west-south-west of Misaoyama were constructed from the end of the fourth century AD with the majority built in the fifth century. From the early shell mounds we can trace the old coastline here precisely. The bay which these tumuli overlook was the largest bay in Kibi and was faced by Kojima Island, the second largest island in the entire Inland Sea. Thus we can see that the seaway along the Bay of Kibi was lined with the impressive mausolea of generations of the Kibi royal families, alerting strangers who sailed by of Kibi's great power. Looking at a map of the ancient coast, surely there was another route which sea traffic between Kyushu and Yamato could have taken? Alas there was not, for south of Kojima near north-western Shikoku is the most treacherous channel in the Inland Sea, including the Naruto whirlpools. Modern tankers avoid this route even today. Therefore, like it or not, the Yamato people depended on the sufferance of Kibi for good relations with Kyushu, Korea and China. The price Yamato paid to keep the sea lanes open must have been enormous and the power of Kibi in those mysterious fourth and fifth centuries unequalled. The Nakayama Chausuyama tumulus and the smaller Kuramayama tumulus nearby are on the border of Bitchu and Bizen, (which were names given to sub-divisions of the Kibi kingdom upon the formation of the Yamato state in the seventh century). To the north, the tombs overlook the Old Sanyo Road with the sea to the south and whether one entered the heart of Kibi on the Soja plain by sea or land these tombs were visible, for the sea then reached the foothills. In Matsunaga Bay, the large tumuli were also by the shore overlooking the seaway and a small estuary. Since there are no plains behind the Matsunaga tumuli, the inference must be that the activities of the occupants of the tombs were concerned with commerce from the sea.

Study of the sea-facing tumuli along the Bay

of Kibi shows that they are similar in style to those further inland. There was an obvious purpose to their strategic positioning along the coast; the rulers of those times were determined to show not only inland power but also coastal supremacy. There are several references to a Kibi navy in both the early Japanese histories. The sailors were probably coastal farmers as well as fishermen and, among the rulers whose tombs line the Kibi coast, some must have taken advantage of the sea traffic and travelled to Korea and even China. Such contact with the politically and culturally advanced Korean peninsula would have placed Kibi in an advantageous position compared with Yamato. It would have resulted in Kibi being a stepping-stone for the introduction of Korean culture to eastern Japan – doubtless a further irritant to the powerful tribes of Yamato. Not only were the Kibi people commercially superior in that they controlled the shipping lanes, but they were also more culturally advanced due to steady Koreanization.

The Chinese, as we know, were well aware of Japan and had written very detailed descriptions of it since the time of the Wei dynasty beginning in the third century. The name the Chinese favoured was Wa – lands of dwarfs. Probably the most controversial mention of Wa is found in the Chinese chronicles of the fifth century where reference to five Wa kings is made in some detail.

Where did the Wa kings rule and what really constituted Wa? Most Japanese scholars opt for Yamato and point out that the tombs of Emperors Ojin, Nintoku, Ritchu, Hanzei and Yuryaku correspond neatly in time and place. They claim that the five Wa kings are the first of the Ojin dynasty which ruled a unified Japan from the fifth century.

I disagree. Wa, in my opinion, describes Japan during Koreanization and those 'countries' referred to as Wa were those states formed by the advance of the Korean people into the Japanese archipelago. This conclusion has also been reached by contemporary Korean historians, who believe that the small Korean kingdom of Kaya, on the southern tip of the peninsula, was a Korean administrative centre controlling the vassal states on the Japanese mainland. We should not lose sight of the fact that the Korean peninsula in the early centuries AD was, like Japan, made up of independent kingdoms of similarly unified clans and tribes. Until the fifth century, individual kingdoms of Japan probably contracted separate arrangements with the various kings of Korea. As both Korean and Japanese histories of the fifth century were written long afterwards, when relations had changed and a unified Japan existed, they vie with each other in explaining which country paid tribute. The Japanese in the *Nihonshoki* are particularly artless in this regard and twist many Korean phrases to suit their own thesis. I think it very likely that the Yamato, Kibi and Kyushu relationships with the peninsula were different. Various reports in the history of Silla (the eastern Korean kingdom) tell of Wa attacks on its territory. These raids were repulsed. Japanese historians believe that the Yamato leaders used the Kibi people, who were more familiar with the sea, as scouts, pilots and sailors whenever they felt inclined to attack Korea. It is possible that isolated Kibi chieftains may have

13. Sunset on the Inland Sea in central Kibi. The island in the foreground, contains the large, raised Kuroshima tumulus, probably for a king of Kibi Shimotsumichi. The position of the tumulus on this island is important, in that the tomb would have been covered with small white stones which reflect the light and would have indicated, to trading vessels sailing by, the power of the nearby community. Such tumuli required enormous labour. Such manpower power could easily be diverted into more sinister pursuits and the site of the tombs are evidence of this.

The kings of Kibi controlled the seas by fear.

cooperated with Yamato's raids but this would hardly have been a policy that the more powerful Kibi ruling families of the fifth century would have encouraged.

Monuments of the Inland Kings

As well as the kings who controlled the commerce through the Inland Sea, ancient Kibi had other powerful lords, as shown by the many tumuli found in the mountain areas. In the fifth century, the rulers of Kibi built enormous tumuli, some as large as the 'imperial' tombs of Yamato, where Nintoku's is the world's largest tomb, surpassing the great pyramids of Egypt. Isolated from the surrounding area by moats, these burial mounds must have been an extraordinary sight. Archaeologists calculate that about two thousand workers, with hoes and straw baskets, would have been required for between fifteen and twenty years to construct a burial mound of such a size. A modern construction company has estimated that with dump trucks, bulldozers and other equipment, King Nintoku's tomb would require twenty-seven months to build at a cost of many millions of American dollars.

There are no examples of tumuli outside Yamato (except in Kibi) constructed in the same style and on the same scale as the Yamato 'imperial' mausolea. It could be that, during the construction of such great tumuli, the Kibi rulers demonstrated their parity with the Yamato rulers. Not surprisingly, we find few stories concerning Kibi at the time of the great tumuli, but today, faced by these gigantic ruins and constant new discoveries, some from simple shell mounds and others from the large tumuli, we must draw some conclusions. A comparison of the numbers of tumuli in Yamato, Kibi and elsewhere is helpful. In Yamato, including all the royal tumuli and the three great tombs of Kings Nintoku, Ritchu and Ojin, there are over forty tombs longer than 100 metres. On Shikoku, there are only two near Takamatsu and on the Japan Sea coast at Izumo, the centre of the Izumo culture, a further two. Similarly, one or two can be found in the provinces next to Yamato. In Kibi, on the other hand, there are over twenty tumuli of this size including two which rank alongside the great tombs of the Yamato rulers.

I attach no special significance to tumuli of a length over 100 metres save the comparative proliferation of such mounds in Kibi. At Kawachi and Izumi in Yamato, the tumuli are connected with the royal family. Kibi, which is quite some distance away, has two enormous tombs. The Tsukuriyama tumulus on the Soja plain between the Takahashi and Asahi Rivers is 350 metres long, and is the fourth largest tomb in Japan. There are only two tumuli in Yamato between 300 and 350 metres long, one being King Keiko's tomb at Kawachi Otsuka and the other the Misei Maruyama tumulus in Kashiwara City. Of the 200 metre long tumuli, most are in Yamato but the Bitchu Sakuzan tomb in Kibi is 270 metres long. The Ryoguzan tumulus at Bizen in Kibi is 180 metres long, while, in the 150 metre range, one or two can be found in each of the other areas against many in Kibi. This comparison of tomb

14. The Tsukuriyama tumulus, keyhole shaped and 360 metres in length. This is the fourth largest tumulus in Japan superseded only by three others in Yamato. Originally this tumulus would have been surrounded by one or possibly two moats. The retainers' tombs could have formed small islands. Clay cylinders have been found studding the circumference on which offerings to the dead were placed. The tomb was built in the traditional three-tiered style, each tier representing heaven, earth and man. The burial chamber was vertical and is inside the rounded end of the tomb. This tumulus has been designated as 'imperial' by the Japanese Imperial Household Agency and therefore cannot be excavated. The contents would be Korean Kayan in style and could well prove the descent of the current imperial family from the early Kayan Puyo conquerors. Tsukuriyama's three larger counterparts are likewise off limits to archaeological excavation and research.

size is compelling evidence that Kibi in the fourth and fifth centuries was a major power.

From a study of the early Totsuki tumuli and their accessories it seems that rule in Kibi was divided. Some followed the Yamato examples; others the native Kibi tradition and style. By the late fourth and early fifth centuries, the tumuli being built were as large as or larger than those in Yamato, with similar style and contents; thus the Kibi chieftains, by this time, were either influencing or being influenced by the tribes of Yamato. That no known examples of objects unique to Kibi such as the earlier *tokushu-kidai* cylinders and offertory trays have been found with the later, larger, tumuli rather supports the latter view. Like the rulers of Yamato, the chieftains of Kibi had become rulers of wider lands. It is, however, essential at this point to understand that the term 'central Yamato government' favoured by Japanese scholars in describing the Yamato political scene of the fifth century is probably an overstatement; I think that it was an assembly of allied chieftains which constantly changed. Kibi, though a local power, would have participated in the Yamato 'government'. The interrelationship between Yamato and Kibi is well illustrated by the fact that *haniwa* with special Kibi characteristics are found on many tumuli in Yamato, and tumuli with strong Yamato features are found in Kibi. Let us now examine the relationship between Kibi and Yamato, relying heavily on guesswork where there is little concrete evidence.

The huge tumuli of Kibi can still be seen today on the alluvial plains, on the mountains and among the rice fields. They are the tombs of chieftains and they represent at least three generations of different families spread over a wide area. Even some of the tumuli of less than 100 metres were of noble origin.

The accompanying chart (prepared by Mr T. Makabe, curator of the Kurashiki Archaeological Museum) shows the chieftains' tumuli stretching from the easternmost border of Kibi to the far west, encompassing the three great river deltas and the smaller rivers between them.

Tumuli shown on the same line on the chart are of the same period. The fourth century tombs are the earliest since their accessories all contain vestiges of the late Yayoi culture. The Kurumazuka tomb on the Asahi River delta is the only exception, since, in size, shape and content, it follows a clear Yamato pattern. The late fourth century tombs, Kekoji and Tenjinyama, on a hilltop on the Oku plain, must be dynastic, since the rounded rear ends of the tumuli containing the burial chambers are adjacent. At about the same time the Urama-Chausuyama, Minato-Chausuyama, Kurumayama (Hanajiri Giri-Giri Yama) and Nakayama tumuli were also constructed. Later, similarly large tumuli were built at other influential communities in Kibi. The general impression remains that, from the late fourth through to the middle fifth centuries, each of the clans was of equal power but they were fewer in number. In the early fifth century, by contrast, three colossal tumuli were constructed on the Takahashi and Ashimori River deltas to the north of Kurashiki City – the Terayama tumulus, 120 metres long, and two others, the names of which are Sakuzan and Tsukuriyama, of 270 and 350 metres in length respectively. On the Sagawa river delta is the Ryoguzan tumulus which is 180 metres long. Tombs of this size are usually only found in Yamato. We cannot tell whether or not the occupants of these great mausolea were from Kibi; they are all very similar in design and appear to be related in pattern to the Yamato royal tombs. With the exception of the Ryoguzan tomb, the three great Takahashi Delta tombs are probably of successive generations of the same family, whose power may have stretched to the west and north, with rivals in eastern Kibi, later the home of the occupant of Ryoguzan tumulus. The conclusion must be that Kibi's greatest era was that of the construction of the Takahashi Ashimori tombs during the early fifth century and that this area was the hub of Kibi.

The Chieftains of Oku

Many of the great tumuli along the Yoshii River in eastern Kibi have been illegally broken open and robbed. Fortunately some of their contents have been traced and are kept in the National Museum in Tokyo. A rectangular stone slab coffin containing two Chinese mirrors from the late Han dynasty (200 BC–AD 200), iron weapons and tools and a bronze and an iron ploughshare (all of which are retained in the National Museum) were all found in the Kekoji tomb (110 metres). At the Tenjinyama tumulus (125 metres) the coffin had been hewn into shape by chisels and lowered into the burial chamber. This coffin contained a stone pillow, and was full of jewels and iron ware (also retained in the National Mu-

seum). Since the two rounded rear ends of both tombs are adjacent to each other, the occupants may have been related. The differing coffins, burial chamber designs, and grave contents, only one with bronze, suggest a rapid transition in the importance of bronze in the area.

The slightly later circular Maruyama tomb (50 metres), which is much smaller than the others, had some unusual contents. Access to the burial chamber was again from the top. The coffin is very finely made in two parts with the lid richly carved with decorative discs and the base well chiselled. More than thirty mirrors were recovered from this tomb, a rare quantity from one tomb even in Yamato but the Maruyama tumulus is the only such tomb outside Yamato.

One of the most puzzling features of the tombs along the Yoshii River is that they were never as large as those elsewhere in Kibi until the end of the fifth century. Then, when in other areas major tomb construction was over, Oku tumuli became larger and more sophisticated. The best example is the Funayama tumulus where the square front portion is very large when compared with the rounded end. In Yamato there is only one other example of this unusual style, the tumulus of King Seinei (AD 444–484), whose half brother was of Kibi blood. The Oku tombs in eastern Kibi also differ from the group in the south-east of the Oku plain at Ushimado and these, in turn, are quite unlike the groups of tumuli found further west.

Tumulus Construction on the Five Kibi River Deltas Late 4th - 5th Century				
Takahashi Ashimori River Delta	Ashimori Sasagase River Deltas	Asahi River Delta	Sagawa River Delta	Yoshii River, Oku Delta
Kozukuriyama 130 m.	Nakayama 150 m.	Kurumazuka 50 m.	Uramachausuyama 120 m.	Kekoji 110 m.
Terayama 120 m.	Doyama 150 m.	Minatochausuyama 150 m.	Koyama 70 m.	Tenjinyama 125 m.
Tsukuriyama (Sakuzan) 270 m.	Komaruyama 150 m.	Sannoyama 70 m.	Tamaimaruyama 140 m.	Maruyama 50 m (circular)
Tsukuriyama 350 m.	Komariyama 100 m. (circular)	Ashinohamachausuyama 80 m.	Ryoguzan 180 m.	Tsukiyama 90 m.
Sensoku 70 m.	Kurumayama 140 m. (Hanajiri Giri Giri Yama)	Kanakuryama 160 m.	Shuzenda 70 m.	Funayama 70 m.
		Jingujiyama 150 m.	Nishimoriyama 100 m .	Ushibumichausuyama 55 m. (scallop shape)
		Ipponmatsu 65 m.		

The River Deltas and the Tumuli of Kibi, 4th - 7th c. A.D.

Tumuli
Other sites

0   5
Miles

BITCHU

BIZEN

Yoshii R.

Asahi R.

Kinojo
Demon's Castle

Ashimori R.

Takahashi R.

Sagawa R.

Ryoguzan
Ashimoriyama

Takashima Shrine

Tamaimaruyama

Tenjinyama

Kurumazuka

Sasagase R.

Kekoji

Komoriyama
Doyama

Urama
Chausyama

Kozukuriyama

Komaruyama

Ushibumi Chausuyama

Tsukuriyama
Senzoku

Tsukiyama

Nakayama
Chausuyama

Jingujiyama

Tsukuriyama
or Sakuzan

Kurumayama

Kanakurayama

Terayama

Koyama

Kibitsu Shrine

Obosan Cemetery

Minatochausuyama

Yoshii
River
Delta

Joto Ruins

Asahi River Delta

Tatetsuki Ruins

Bay
of Kibi

Takashima
Shrine

to/from Korea

to/from Yamato

Ushimado
Bay

Harima
Channel

KOJIMA
ISLAND

Yugasan

SHODOSHIMA

Kibi's Iron Grip

On some hills in the Asahi River delta near the modern city of Okayama are three similar tumuli built between the end of the fourth and the beginning of the fifth century. The Minato Chausuyama tumulus and the nearby Kanakurayama tomb face the sea. Looking southward from the rounded end of the Kanakurayama tumulus, the view is identical with that from Minato Chausuyama. The Bay of Kibi then extended into the hills on which these tumuli are positioned, affording a superb view of the eastern sea entrance to Kibi. Journeying into Kibi from this eastern entrance we would then have been confronted with an island in the centre of the seaway; on this island, known today as Takashima, relics of religious festivals dating from the fifth century have been found. From these and the position of the two tombs it is clear that the eastern entrance was of great strategic importance to the Kibi chieftains of the fifth century.

When the Kanakurayama tumulus was surveyed and examined some years ago, it was confirmed that it had been robbed many years before. The survey did, however, uncover a sub-chamber to the existing two vertical stone-lined chambers in the rounded rear end. The sub-chamber contained four dome-lidded pottery boxes full of iron tools. The manner in which the boxes had been placed and the selection of the tools clearly indicates the significance of iron in fifth century Kibi. The third tomb called Jingujiyama is in the centre of the plain, on the banks of the Asahi River, and today is surrounded by houses. Like the Kanakurayama tomb, it had been robbed but again a later survey uncovered a sub-chamber which contained quantities of iron implements, many of which had been damaged by the robbers.

Perhaps the most significant discovery in the tombs of this early fifth century period was made at a small tomb called Sakakiyama, which I believe to be a retainer's tomb, in the front of the great Tsukuriyama tumulus (350 metres). Within recent memory basket loads of iron were removed from it, again supporting the theory that Kibi was then abundantly rich in iron. Some horse-shaped bronze belt buckles were also recovered from the Sakakiyama tomb. Such buckles were made in Korea; these are the only examples found in Japan, and they are currently held by the Imperial Household Agency at the Tokyo National Museum.

The iron recovered from the Kanakurayama tumulus was mostly forged, but among the iron implements were five axe heads which had been cast. Many axe heads of similar style have been found in Korea and therefore we can be almost certain that these cast objects were imported. Very few similar objects have been found in Japan but, interestingly, some were found on Okinoshima, the Island of the Gods, in the middle of the Genkai Straits separating Japan and Korea. Korean objects are not rare on this small sacred island (where women are prohibited) and even ancient Persian and Indian, as well as Chinese and Japanese, artifacts have been found. The Japanese have always considered that the isolated island of Okinoshima and its three shrines was the site of a Japanese rite to pray for

15. Precious iron objects in a well-crafted domed box from the Kanakurayama tumulus. Pottery boxes of this style are extremely rare. It is possible that the occupant of the tomb may have been involved in the iron industry or was responsible for the fledgling local production which gradually replaced imported material. Iron was possibly first smelted in Kibi in the late fourth century.

The Kurashiki Archeological Museum.

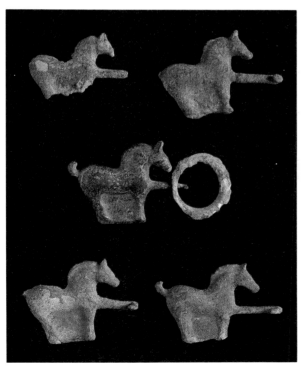

16. Korean bronze horse-shaped belt buckles excavated at the Sakakiyama tumulus, a retainer's tomb in front of the enormous Tsukuriyama tumulus (see plate 14). Similar buckles have been found in Korea and are of Scythian influence. It is fairly certain that these buckles were imported, for such craftsmanship would not have been possible in fourth century Kibi. The possibility, however, that they are the work of imported Korean artisans exists.

The Imperial Household Agency, Tokyo.

a safe crossing to Korea. This may have been so at the time of the writing of the early histories, but I believe that in the fourth and fifth centuries, Okinoshima was a Korean shrine linked with Kaya. It would have been the last stop for prayer on the journey from Korea to Japan, and later Japanese historians have inverted the significance of the shrines to suit their xenophobic prejudices. That similar objects have been found both in Kibi and Okinoshima suggests a strong connection between Kibi and Korea. Similar links are well accepted in northern Kyushu, where Korean treasure from the Eta-Funayama tumulus has been related to pieces found under stones on Okinoshima. My earlier contention that Kaya was a Korean office for the control of vassal states on the Japanese mainland is further supported by these discoveries from the Kanakurayama and Sakakiyama tumuli in Kibi. It also seems to me significant, if not a trifle sinister, that some of the undoubtedly Korean objects found near the great Tsukuriyama tumulus in Kibi, though not necessarily of 'Imperial' origin, should be in the safe-keeping of the Imperial Household Agency.

Relations between the Kibi Royal Family and the Yamato Court

The Chinese references to the 'five kings of Wa' and their foreign relations, appear at the same time as the great mausolea of Kibi were being constructed for the powerful Kibi kings who ordered them in the early fifth century. These ref-erences are particularly noteworthy since the first Japanese histories of the eighth century make no mention of any such foreign relations between the five consecutive kings between Ojin and Yuryaku, whose dates, with relevant cycle corrections, correspond roughly to those referred to by the Chinese (AD 413–502). Naturally the names used by the Chinese and Japanese scholars do not correspond and endless discussion has taken place to determine which of the Chinese references relates to a Japanese source. The safest method may be to compare the posthumous names and lineage in the Japanese writings with the Chinese chronicles and sources.

Tentatively, emphasizing the loaded Japanese argument, the chronology of the 'dynasty' would read: (Chinese names first) San (Nintoku), Chin (Hanzei), Sai (Ingyo), Ko (Ankyo), Bu (Yuryaku). The first Chinese reference, in AD 413, to 'Wa barbarians' corresponds with the reign of the Japanese King Ritchu. The Chinese records depict the 'five kings of Wa' as tributary monarchs and describe in detail the political relationship between 'Wa' and China over a ninety-year period from AD 413, including exchanges of envoys, presentations of gifts and dates of death and succession. Probably the most curious reference is to the Wa kings' constant requests for Chinese titles and recognition. Comparing these requests with Korean records it is clear that the Japanese Wa kings sought to present themselves as superior to their Korean neighbours. One such request from Japanese Wa actually asked for the Korean kingdom of Paekche (previously founded by the Puyo) to be referred to as a Yamato protectorate; this was refused. It seems quite clear that the Wa kings and the other Korean kingdoms vied with each other in a mutually submissive attitude to China. China's evaluation of Wa was, in the event, not very flattering.

For me, this indicates how the Chinese bureaucratic system of government slowly established itself among the clan and tribal societies of Korea and Japan. Study of the Japanese tumuli and regional dynastic overtones shows that the system, unlike the Chinese, was basically aristocratic. Clan chieftains and tribal leaders were given new titles in the Chinese style, but real power remained with the old families with land and a history, rather than a 'government rank'. The Chinese system, moreover, would have unified the aristocracy with a royal family at its head.

The Japanese scholar Hirano Kunio has magnanimously suggested that some of the 'five kings of Wa' bestowed the Chinese title of 'General' on their vassals with the consent of the Chinese emperor and that the chieftains of Kibi were possibly among the recipients. I would suggest that it is by no means certain from where the 'five kings of Wa' ruled, nor that, by this stage, any authoritative power had been established over the local chieftains. Both the early eighth century Japanese histories go to great lengths to describe the deaths and burial places of the kings, best corresponding with the Chinese records, of the 'five kings of Wa', but they are not in agreement on the reign of the eighteenth King Hanzei. The *Kojiki* makes no reference to him whatsoever. It is this disputed King Hanzei, with the Chinese name Chin, who requested titles for his vassal states, of which Kibi may have been one.

Both Japanese histories are notoriously unreliable and therefore I see no reason why it should be accepted that the 'five kings of Wa' ruled from Yamato or that the Chinese records refer to a dynasty. As I have often mentioned, the term Wa – 'lands of dwarfs' – had been in use since the early third century. I am inclined to the Korean theory that the centre of power of Wa was at Kaya on the Korean peninsula and that the Wa on the Japanese mainland were merely Koreanized branch states in which Kibi or part of Kibi was represented. It is quite possible that the later Puyo/Kayan rulers of Yamato maintained direct relations with China and tried to have their old Korean dominions regarded by Chinese title and address as their protectorates; however, the Chinese probably chose to see no distinction and grouped them all together as barbarians. It is possible that, at a later date, Kibi paid tribute to China and that its ruler received a Chinese title. Again, the Chinese would have made no distinction and would have included Kibi in their overall view of Wa, thus conforming to the later logical and sophisticated Korean (Paekche) explanation of a continuing structure of branch states answerable to royal Puyo/Kayan conquerors. I further believe that at the time between the construction of the two great tumuli of Kibi and the so-called 'imperial' tumuli of Yamato in the fifth century, Kibi and Yamato were rivals and that for a time Kibi, through its control of the seaway to Korea (and therefore the distribution of iron), was the more powerful, until a Puyo /Kayan/Kibi conquest of Yamato established a central court at Yamato. Kibi would have been part of Wa for a considerable time; a constant stream of mainland immigrants, having established the most eastwardly sophisticated state in Wa, then gradually unified the regional Kibi rulers under the rule of a single family. That this Kibi supremacy was short-lived is not in debate and I accept that eventually Kibi was later defeated by a more powerful Yamato hegemony.

The purpose of my thesis is to place Kibi correctly within Japanese history and to debunk some of the xenophobic historical theories about Japan and Korea. The final battle for Kibi must have been fast, bloody and decisive. It probably took place during the late fifth century, when a unified Wa attacked the eastern Korean kingdom of Silla with a 'fleet of a hundred troopships' and more than half the Wa invasion force was destroyed before it was repulsed.

It is likely that, during the first half of the fifth century, the pattern of gradual unification of the country changed. We can read accounts in both the early histories of military expeditions against the eastern and western barbarians. A study of these expeditions shows that peace was rare, so a more diplomatic solution may have been sought to subdue the powers of Kibi, and remedy found in exogamy, or marriage outside the clan. Intermarriage between the two most powerful families of Kibi and Yamato naturally resulted in a softening of the fierce chauvinism which had characterized each. We shall therefore examine this theory from an historical and archaeological viewpoint and test its validity.

The Archaeological Evidence

At the beginning of the Tumulus period, the tumulus styles in Yamato and Kibi were very different. There was a gradual cross-fertilization until ultimately the Yamato style prevailed. As we have seen, the distribution of tumuli indicates a change from the old custom of a tribal patriarch being buried among his people as one of the tribe, to the emergence of a ruling class commanding the energies of the people to construct tumuli and provide rich tomb accessories for an aristocratic afterlife.

In comparing the tombs of Kibi and Yamato, we can see that even though the number of great tumuli in Kibi over 100 metres in length is impressive, it is surpassed by the great tumuli of Yamato. Before the construction of the colossal tombs of Kings Nintoku, Ojin and Ritchu at Kawachi, there had probably been a royal family at Miwa in Yamato, for numerous tombs of over 200 metres have been found there. It therefore seems that, between the mid and late fourth century, Kibi was in a different league from Miwa. But even so the rulers of Kibi were still able to build tombs similar to the later Yamato kings in size, style and adornment. It is significant that this happened nowhere else, for it means that the occupants of the two huge tombs in Kibi might have predated their Yamato counterparts and yet have been allies, and may even have been related to each other. Their possible influence and links with Korea have been demonstrated but I must again stress the significance of the Korean horse-shape buckles in the retainer's tomb.

17. A Chokkomon design carved stone screen inside the Senzoku tumulus, possibly a retainer's tomb close to the giant Tsukuriyama tumulus in central Kibi. This Chokkomon design is also found in Kyushu and serves to illustrate the eastern path of cultural influence into Kibi in the late fourth or early fifth century when this tomb is believed to have been constructed.

18. *Myoto-iwa* style (husband and wife) stones at the Suga shrine, Soja City, central Kibi. They commemorate the union of King Nintoku of Yamato and Princess Kuro the grand-daughter of Prince Kibitsu-Hiko. *Miyoto-iwa* are a type of Shinto shrine and the two rocks are often attached by rice straw ropes, demonstrating union. There are many similar rocks in Kibi. These monuments however, are not ancient, and are replacements of earlier, carved stones.

At the Senzoku tumulus, another of the retainers' tombs in front of the great Tsukuriyama tomb, a large, well-chiselled and shapely rectangular stone screen with deeply carved 'Chokkomon' design was placed across the horizontal chamber to prevent the dead spirit from escaping. Elsewhere, this is only found in the northern Kyushu tumuli and serves as a further indication of the western inclination of Kibi at this very important time.

One cannot be certain whether the occupants of the great Tsukuriyama tomb ruled Kibi to its far boundaries, since contemporaneous large tumuli were also built in outlying areas. If they were the sovereign kings of Kibi, then they certainly had some very powerful local chieftains in their fiefdom. The only common feature of all the tombs, including Tsukuriyama, is that they all show an original Yamato influence in their design and contents.

Princess Kuro of Kibi

The well-rehearsed unreliability of the eighth century histories is further illustrated by their treatment of a poignant story concerning a Kibi princess, a granddaughter of Prince Kibitsu-Hiko and a Yamato king. The *Kojiki* tells the story in its chapters on King Nintoku. The *Nihonshoki* connects the tale with the earlier King Ojin. It concerns Princess Kuro, the beautiful daughter of the sovereign of Kibi, who was taken by the king as his mistress and later bore him children. Her beauty was such that when she arrived in Yamato, the queen was moved to rages of jealousy which became so fierce that the Kibi princess 'fled to her native land' by boat. Upon her departure, the heartbroken king composed a poem in which he referred to Princess Kuro as his wife; on hearing of this the queen was further enraged and sent minions to chase the princess ashore and force her to return home by foot. Then the king, on the pretext of a royal hunt on the island of Awaji, hastened after the princess and, passing the island of Shodoshima, entered Kibi and visited the sovereign of Kibi at 'the palace at Ashimori'. It is recorded in the *Nihonshoki* that on his second visit to Kibi, the king 'removed his dwelling to Ashimori'. Princess Kuro's father was the sovereign of Kibi, named as Mitomo-Wake, the son of Prince Kibitsu-Hiko. In the *Nihonshoki* it is recorded that he served the king well and that he, in return, divided Kibi up and 'granted it in fee' to Mitomo-Wake's children. A lengthy description of those divisions is given; the district of the Hatori-be (weavers) was granted to Princess Kuro and the *Nihonshoki* then proclaims: 'wherefore his [the king's] children dwell to this day in the land of Kibi'.

This story, common to both the early histories, shows how the Yamato kings came to terms with Kibi through exogamy. The sovereigns of Kibi appear later and assume an even more interesting role than royal fathers-in-law. The list of names of Mitomo-Wake's family and their spheres of influence in Kibi should not be overstressed, nor should the royal division of Kibi. These are understandable attempts by a later Yamato court to boost its own image and superiority; Kibi descendants probably held powerful positions in Yamato in the eighth century and

concessions to fact had to be made.

It is not difficult to imagine the Kibi kings sending their navies into the Genkai Straits and controlling the sea trade between Korea, Kyushu and Yamato, though at the time of the great tombs this force would have been, for the main part, on the defensive. It is also simple to visualize the wealth accumulated from such commerce, directed toward labour forces of tens of thousands carrying rocks and earth to build the enormous burial mounds ordered during the lifetime of their ultimate occupants. In the light of this, it seems unlikely that the sovereigns of Kibi would have allowed their women to join the Yamato courts as mere 'mistresses'. Such 'imperial' historical misrepresentations make little sense, when in the same chronicles these 'mistresses' take off at will for their homelands and kings follow them; it would be far too naive to put all this down to love. Reading between the lines, it seems fairly clear that the Yamato kings had to be very careful in their relationships with the Kibi chieftains. In a short space of one hundred years, however, the stories concerning the chieftains of Kibi changed completely.

Sakitsuya, King of Kibi by the Sea

In the *Nihonshoki* there are two stories concerning a king of coastal Kibi. In the seventh year (AD 463) of the reign of the Yamato King Yuryaku (AD 418–479) one of the officers of the royal guard in Yamato, who was from the bowmans' guild in Kibi, known as 0-sora, had to return to his homeland for a private reason and went with royal consent. King Sakitsuya of coastal Kibi detained the officer for several months and would not allow him to return to Yamato. When King Yuryaku heard about this he was furious and promptly sent a servant to fetch his officer. King Sakitsuya then released him and he was able to return to his position with the royal guard, but told King Yuryaku of King Sakitsuya's contempt for him. According to the officer, the Kibi king formed, for his private amusement, armies of females to fight each other. Young girls were dressed as soldiers in Yuryaku's colours, and older women in Sakitsuya's colours. If at any stage the young girls looked as if they were likely to win, King Sakitsuya flew into a maniacal rage and slew them.

A further story also illustrates the Kibi king's contempt for King Yuryaku. This told of Sakitsuya taking a small rooster which he called Yuryaku; plucking out its feathers and clipping its wings, he then matched it in a contest against a huge bird called by his own name, to which he had attached bells and sharp spurs. If the smaller rooster were to appear the stronger, he would draw his sword and kill it. When King Yuryaku heard these stories he was naturally greatly annoyed and sent 'thirty soldiers to Kibi'. They promptly put King Sakitsuya and seventy of his household to death.

Though it may be a blatant fabrication by the later Yamato historians, this story shows that the attitude of Yamato was steadily changing; there are strong overtones of severe competition and fighting between Kibi and Yamato which gives credibility to my theory of there having been a final bloody showdown.

Tasa, King of Eastern Kibi

Perhaps the most poignant and the most important reference to Kibi in the *Nihonshoki* is the tale of Princess Waka, the wife of Tasa, king of Kibi Kamitsumichi. Tasa, his wife and their descendants are, I believe, the most significant personalities from Kibi recorded in the *Nihonshoki* and there is little doubt that they lived. In the light of recent archaeological discoveries the proper interpretation of this story is vital, for in it the essence of Kibi's position, its power and relationships with Korea and Yamato are exposed, and this in the very words of the imperial historians of the eighth century, who were determined to have Kibi's proper role written out and lost forever. Without the archaeological findings the story would be meaningless. The inclusion of the story suggests that Tasa's descendants, or his wife's, were living and powerful at the time of the compilation of the *Nihonshoki* and must have insisted on its being told, albeit in a watered-down version.

Rumours of the extraordinary beauty of Princess Waka reached the palace of the Yamato King Yuryaku. The king decided to make her one of his concubines, but in order to clear the way, he appointed King Tasa governor of Kaya (in Korea); during Princess Waka's marriage to Tasa she bore him two sons, Yehimi and Otokimi.

Soon after taking up his position as governor of Kaya, Tasa learnt that the Yamato king had married his wife. Clearly intending to attack the king and Yamato, Tasa journeyed to Silla, the mortal enemy of Yamato, to seek reinforcements for a combined Kaya and Kibi army attack against King Yuryaku. On hearing of Tasa's move, King Yuryaku immediately commanded Tasa's son Otokimi and Awako-Kibi-no-Amano-Atahe – thought to be an allusion to Kibi's naval power – to attack and punish Silla.

Otokimi set off with a large force and reached Paekche, but never actually attacked Silla. With a group of artisans given in tribute by Paekche, he settled on a large island for several months. His father, Tasa, was so delighted that he had chosen not to attack Silla that he encouraged Otokimi to return to Paekche and work towards destroying its relations with Yamato while he, Tasa, did the same in Kaya. Otokimi's wife, Princess Kusu, however, was loyal to King Yuryaku and so murdered her husband, remaining on the island with Awako-Kibi-no-Amano-Atahe and the Paekche artisans.

Otokimi had failed, but King Yuryaku was still determined to conquer Silla and commissioned an aged general named Ki-no-Oyumi (Ki province was between Kibi and Yamato) to lead the attack. He awarded him an *uneme*, a 'female palace attendant'; these girls were usually chosen for their beauty and were often, according to the early historians, daughters of district governors from Kibi, while this particular one was probably senior lady-in-waiting to Princess Waka (Tasa's wife). She followed the Ki general into battle, attended him, and after he had fallen ill and died in Korea, accompanied the body back to Japan, where she presented herself to the court and demanded that a proper mausoleum be erected. The king granted her wish and personally appointed a funeral committee at the head of which he placed his chief minister. The lady-in-waiting later presented six Korean slaves to the minister as a token of her appreciation.

Princess Waka had two other sons, both fathered by King Yuryaku and named Iwaki and Hoshikawa. After the king's death, Princess Waka encouraged her younger son, Hoshikawa, to claim the Yamato throne. She advised him to secure the treasury first. His elder brother counselled against what was virtually a coup d'état, but his advice was not heeded. Hoshikawa attacked the treasury, took possession of it and 'exercised arbitrary authority and squandered official property'. The chief minister, in association with the Yamato titled families wishing to enthrone Yuryaku's chosen heir, raised a force and attacked the treasury, blockaded it and set it on fire. Inside were Princess Waka, Princes Iwaki, Hoshikawa and another son of Princess Waka (by a different father, Prince Anikimi). All were 'roasted to death'.

When the princes of upper Kibi heard that civil war was taking place in Yamato, they dispatched a fleet of forty warships to aid their half brother Hoshikawa, but they heard the news of his defeat while still off the coast and returned to Kibi without landing. Later the newly-enthroned King Seinei (reigned AD 480–484) summoned the princes of upper Kibi and dispossessed them of their domains in the mountains of Kibi.

From these several stories recorded in the

Nihonshoki we can gain an impression of the power of Kibi in the fifth century. They were obviously written from a Yamato viewpoint and at imperial command, so they are naturally slanted to favour Yamato and inflate its royal prestige. In my view it is particularly important to assess Princess Waka's position with great care. It is appropriate to view her, in the light of the Korean association, as the personification of 'Wa' marrying into Yamato. It is possible that Tasa was, in fact, the son of one of the kings of Kaya and governor of Kibi, a branch state of Wa, whose wife then married King Yuryaku and bore him two sons of part-old, part-new Korean royal blood.

In the story of the coup d'état, therefore, we can envisage a Kibi attempt for the Yamato throne. The episode in the story describing the seizing of the treasury could be a deliberate distortion of the truth, in which, more likely, Prince Hoshikawa, together with his powerful Kibi mother, had succeeded in usurping the throne. The old Yamato chieftains were then obviously divided in their loyalty and civil war broke out. Hoshikawa and his mother, realizing the gravity of the situation, summoned to their aid the Kibi navy, controlled by their relatives, but they were too late. The Yamato chieftains moved faster, toppled the usurpers and 'roasted them' in their palace.

One of the easiest mistakes made today, when reading ancient history like the *Nihonshoki*, is to forget the time that journeys took. From Yamato to Kibi and back would have taken at least two weeks, the assembly and outfitting of a navy very much longer. I think, therefore, that

Kibi power ruled in Yamato for at least a year. But prior to Yuryaku's death, Princess Waka must have been the most powerful lady in Yamato. King Yuryaku appointed a crown prince, by another mother, only one year before his death. This implies that almost throughout his reign of nearly a quarter of a century, Kibi influence on the Yamato court was dominant and during this period the chieftains of Kibi would have had little opposition from Yamato. When a coastal chieftain such as King Sakitsuya rebelled against a central Kibi authority, he was probably put down by a combination of central Kibi and Yamato forces.

To me, it is hardly a coincidence that the style of the tumulus in Yamato of King Seinei (reigned AD 480–484), Yuryaku's designated crown prince, is identical to the Funayama tumulus on the Oku plain in Kibi, from where King Tasa ruled and whence Princess Waka, later King Yuryaku's wife, is alleged to have come. King Seinei and Prince Hoshikawa were half-brothers. The inclusion of the superfluous account of the Kibi lady-in-waiting, presenting Korean slaves to King Yuryaku's chief minister, is a further indication of Yamato's acceptance of Kibi's superior relations with Korea. It is also interesting to note that the aged general sent by Yuryaku to attack Silla came from the province of Ki. Ki also possessed a powerful navy and Yuryaku's choice of the Ki general Ki-no-Oyumi to lead the attack is an indication of Yamato's weakness on the sea. The fact that the Ki general was sent, rather than one from Kibi, suggests that the Kibi sea kings had formed an alliance elsewhere—with King Tasa and the King of Kaya?

CHAPTER V

Sunset and a New Faith

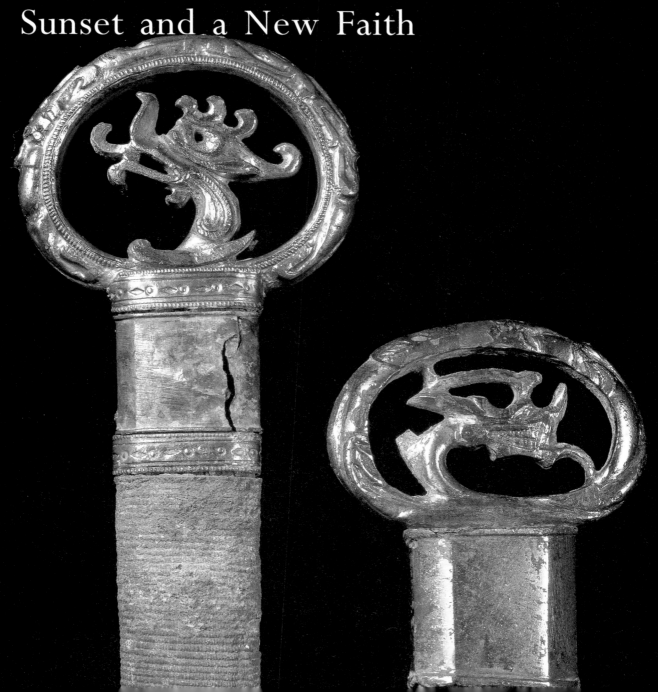

The most visible evidence of the importance of Kibi during the fourth and fifth centuries is in the hundreds of tumuli which are found along its coastline, on hills overlooking the sea, further inland among the rice fields, and on the delta plains. All serve to show that a large and important civilization flourished but was deliberately forgotten by later historians. It is much more difficult, however, to gain an impression of communal life in those days since there are few sites which could reveal that background. From those available the only clues derive from the pit dwellings, ruins and the debris found among them. Certainly a very sophisticated form of society existed, but unlike the Chinese, the Japanese social structure followed the Korean, and was hereditary and aristocratic. Power lay in the hands of the old families with land or commercial monopolies, rather than stemming from a government rank. Both the early histories describe society as it then existed and the social make-up of the communities is covered in great detail. A system of *be* ('guilds') had been introduced along Korean patterns, with slaves and retainers subservient to them; the *be* in turn answered to minor nobles and then the aristocracy. The *be* embodied a wide range of trades, and employment, within one, became hereditary.

Almost every occupation was represented by a *be*; weavers, carpenters, potters, embroiderers, printers, and fishermen, etc. Traces of these guilds can still be found today in that many Japanese family names carry *be* as a suffix, suggesting the hereditary nature of the system. As to the military organization, it is not difficult to deduce from the tombs that the king was supported by lesser aristocrats as staff and senior officers. Unlike the Chinese, the sprigs of the aristocracy devoted their time almost exclusively to military training. Land ownership was regularized by royal grant to officials who used slaves captured in frequent local wars to clear and work the land. Many gifts of slaves are recorded, emphasizing the importance of slaves within the social structure and Kibi was rich in labour, while free farmers were taxed and subject to military conscription as, no doubt, were fishermen.

The fourth and fifth centuries were times of great social change. As the tribal leagues matured into kingdoms and relations between the Wa states and other Korean kingdoms strengthened, so the pressure to emulate the cultural sophistication of the mainland peninsula became greater. In both the eighth century histories there are constant references to the movement of skilled craftsmen from China and Korea to Japan and these 'naturalized' immigrant artisans probably headed the *be*. Unlike today, there was thus little social stigma attached to being a foreigner and when a census was taken it was found that virtually all the Yamato aristocracy proudly claimed Korean ancestry. Instances of members of different Korean royal families settling in Japan are numerous, and intermarriage would have been commonplace. As one of the most important stepping stones for the introduction of mainland culture into east Japan, Kibi would have absorbed many Korean settlers and possessed a military or social system very like the Korean original.

The contents of many of the tombs excavated in Kibi and further west on Kyushu are vital to

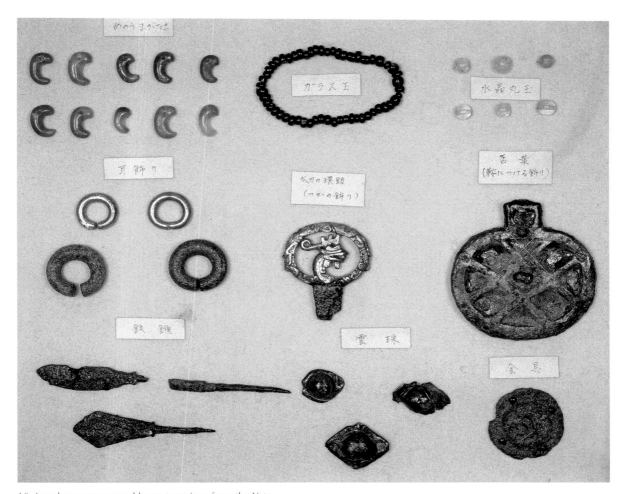

めのう まがたま

ガラス玉

水晶丸玉

耳飾り

太刀の環頭
(つかの飾り)

舌葉
(鞍につける飾り)

鈇鑁

雲珠

金具

19. Jewelry, weapons and horse trappings from the Yata tumulus in central Kibi. The comma shaped beads or *magatama* represent bear claws and were made from valuable stones such as jade, chalcedony and agate, and also of glass. These beads are found only in Korea and Japan. They were strung as necklaces, worn singly and wired to gold crowns and diadems. Often they were sewn onto clothing. The wearing of such claws symbolized the powers of animals which humans lacked.

Kibi Shrine.

an understanding of fourth and fifth century art and craftsmanship. A fabulous array of gold bracelets, earrings, belts, pendants and glass vessels has been recovered from the many tombs which have been investigated. These demonstrate great artistic competence and illustrate the luxurious life of the aristocracy. Very few of these pieces, however, were manufactured locally; they are largely imported from the Korean peninsula. The design of much of the jewelry provides precious information about the myths and shaman mysticism surrounding the contemporary view of the universe. Many objects, particularly the Korean horse-shaped belt buckles found in the Sakakiyama tumulus, point clearly to the influence of Scythian art common to the early nomadic Euro-Asian tribal communities who so greatly influenced all parts of Korea. The ancient Koreans believed that animals were closely akin to men and that the universe consisted of three worlds; Heaven, Earth and the Kingdom of the Dead, also known as the Water World.

When the Kanakurayama tumulus in eastern Kibi was excavated, several pottery representations of water birds were discovered as was also a finely modelled cock's head. The ancient people of Kaya adorned their dead in birds' feathers; their shamans believed that the dead would be transformed into flying creatures as soon as they placed wings upon their backs. The rooster symbolized the sun to both the early Korean and the Japanese people and in Korea rooster wings were used for ritually decorative purposes. The significance of birds in fourth and fifth century Japanese society and the adoption of Kayan practices is exemplified by a Japanese-manufactured bronze alloy crown discovered at Yoshino, near Nara. It bore traces of birds' wings on it, implying that the Korean bird cult spread as far east as Yamato, presumably via Kibi.

One of the objects most frequently recovered from both graves and tumuli is a small comma-shaped jewel bead called a *magatama*. The *magatama* played an important role as a talisman; such beads have also been found in ancient Jomon sites but few in Yayoi ruins. They are believed to have their origins in Siberia and their incidence spread down the Korean peninsula from the Altai Mountains, whence the original Shaman and Shinto religious beliefs emanated. This mystical cult was based on the relationship between men and animals. The *magatama* jewels represent the claws of bears and other wild animals; on the Korean peninsula such wild beasts were objects of worship. The plant world is represented in the form of tiny metal-shaped discs on the crowns found in west Japan and it is no coincidence that Korean documents describe how the Paekche kings wore crowns decorated with gold and silver flowers.

The nether world, water world or kingdom of the dead, might well be represented by the moats which surround the tombs, the zigzag pattern symbolizing waves found on many crowns and later as paper streamers hanging at Shinto shrines—still seen today. The common religious symbolism of the early written histories of both Korea and Japan, supported by similar graphic devices, underlines the strength of peninsular influences on fourth and fifth century Wa.

Buildings in Kibi, like those in other kingdoms, were generally made of wood and so have not survived. From numerous well-modelled pottery *haniwa* found all over Japan, however, it is possible to gain some insight into the architectural methods of the time.

The early social unit in Kibi was a clan or the union of several families into a community later termed *uji*. The *uji* had a common family and place name and the name given to their settlements was *mura*, which originally meant 'a group'. The broader term encompassing the surrounding rice land and the people was *kuni*. In Kibi and elsewhere the *uji* had guardian gods in the form of rocks or trees. The *uji* were ruled both politically and religiously by a chief known as *uji-no-kami*. *Uji-no-kami* gradually became clan chieftains. The later need for greater unification for rice cultivation and protection made the *uji-no-kami* powerful political and religious symbols as kings of emerging nations. In Kibi, as we have seen, there were several such emerging nations, until one king ultimately became paramount.

This gradual consolidation of power is seen in the construction of larger and larger tumuli which involved the collective labour of thousands upon thousands of people. The *haniwa* give a fairly clear impression of how the people dressed. The styles are predictably similar to those of Korea and in the case of the nobility the court costume was almost identical. Women wore close-fitting jackets tied left over right, with tight sleeves, and skirts were pleated and flared in the Korean style. Necklaces were popular; while young girls wore their hair long, elder married women cropped their hair and relied more on combs. Wrist, ear and neck ornaments

Korea at that time

Buddhism spread from China to the northern kingdom of Koguryo in the early-mid fourth century AD. The form of Buddhism popular in China was Mahayana, a doctrine which involved Bodhisattvas or persons who had achieved Buddhahood and had helped the suffering to achieve Nirvana—a state of enlightenment. Because Buddhism was not a threat to government and supported the monarchy, it spread quickly. It mixed well with the old popular beliefs and soon became the mainstay of the bureaucracy and the means by which education was spread to the people. Chinese and Korean contemporary records tell of the construction of many beautiful temples and exchanges of scholars and monks.

Within two decades Mahayana Buddhism was also introduced to the Kingdom of Paekche and, with it, stronger cultural ties with China were forged. At the time of the Puyo/Kayan conquest of Japan (AD 369) Buddhism had a firm hold in Korea, and it is inconceivable that the doctrines of the new religion did not spread to Japan at the same time. The king of Paekche had embraced Buddhism and as in Koguryo, temples were constructed on a massive scale and the adoption of Chinese culture into a local form continued. Hundreds of Buddhist monks arrived from China and helped in the dissemination of the new faith in all directions – even further east to the populous tribes of western Japan.

Mention of such religious envoys are numerous in the Japanese Kojiki and Nihonshoki histories. The dates, however, have been tampered with and distorted for reasons only truly known to the early historians. A probable reason would be to place less emphasis on outside influences and to demonstrate that the order of things was directed from Yamato, not Paekche, and that relations between China and Japan did not require third country participation. This was probably the case in the eighth century but certainly not in the fourth, when everything new came from Paekche – new government, new culture, new medicine, along with a new people who also carried the new faith with them across the sea to Kyushu and later to Kibi and Yamato.

20. Gold earrings probably imported from Kaya in Korea; fourth–fifth century AD, excavated in Kibi. Such flower petal-shaped beads are common in Korea but rare in Kibi. Such ostentatious jewelry was unpopular with the ancient Chinese but the people of Korea had a passion for hanging ornaments which jingled. The filigree work on some is magnificent and of the highest quality. Carry-overs of this fashion can also be found on stoneware ceramics in both Korea and Japan where elaborate decoration was attached with finely made ceramic chains. Representations of birds, flowers, hearts and discs were all the rage and variations were worn by both male and female.

The Okayama Prefectural Museum.

21. Korean-Kayan style iron armour excavated from the Zuian tumulus, Soja City in central Kibi; fifth century AD. This chest armour is completely Kayan in style; it was probably for a foot soldier. Almost identical armour has been excavated in Korea and there is a fine example in the Kyemyong Museum in Taegu, Korea. There are many examples of this armour found on *haniwa*, the clay tomb figurines used to protect the ancient tumuli.

The Soja City Office.

22. Gilt bronze sword hilts inspired by Korean-Kayan styles, believed to have been manufactured in Kibi; if so, probably by immigrant craftsmen. Excavated from the Iwata tumulus no. 14, western Kibi. The style of these hilts originated in Han China and the long single-edged blade was much preferred by the Kibi warriors over the short sword because of its obvious psychological advantages. It was not long before these imported style swords were abstracted in design and took on characteristics unique to Japan, but retaining vestiges of the Chinese originals.

The Sanyo Town Office.

23. A reconstructed peasant's dwelling of the late Yayoi period, third century AD, Hinase, eastern Kibi. Similar thatched dwellings of the ordinary people were dotted all over Kibi. The wealthy constructed their houses from wood using the precious imported iron tools to cut the timber.

Photo: The Hinase City Office

embodied stylized bear claws and flowers. Men, who appear more frequently in *haniwa* form, are usually shown in court and military uniforms. Court dress was long robed and included jewelry with earrings, wrist-bells and hair ornaments. The hair was plaited in pigtails, often decorated with ribbons; soldiers wore baggy trousers and iron, wood and leather armour. On some of the *haniwa* are detailed representations of the well equipped soldier carrying sword, quiver and shield. *Haniwa* representations of the servile classes include musicians carrying instruments, actors, clowns and household servants bearing food. It seems from many *haniwa* that facial decoration (tattooing) was popular, as were hats; crowns decorated in the Korean style with *magatama* and discs are also quite common. *Haniwa* models of storehouses and dwellings

found in northern Kyushu and along the Inland Sea should give a fair impression of Kibi architecture. A bronze mirror of the early fifth century, discovered near Nara, illustrates four houses and gives, in my opinion, the best indication of the types of building to be found in an urban community of the time.

From this mirror we can see how the old pit dwelling of Yayoi times was still used by the common people, the thatched roof extended to the ground and there are no walls. A line on the left of the building suggests that the door could be raised. Another building has a gabled roof, and rests on the ground like the conventional farmers' houses of today. The other two houses are on stilts and one is probably the home of a chieftain; a parasol, a sign of high rank, supports this theory; this house has a balcony and three

24. Wall ruins of the Demon's Castle complex, built by Korean immigrants in the seventh century AD. Evidence of the earliest occupation date from the Jomon period, third century BC. Archaeological digging has unearthed evidence of vast storehouses and artifacts from many periods. It is most likely that this castle is the palace of 'Emperors' Nintoku or Ojin at Ashimori in Kibi, referred to in the eighth century histories. Both are said to have married the granddaughter of Kibitsu-Hiko and to have lived in Kibi for some years.

bays. The other building on stilts is either a storehouse or a shrine; it has two bays and is strikingly similar to the main building of the Izumo Shrine. These four buildings reflect very neatly the functional and social characteristics of the period. Obviously the construction work required an extensive use of iron. The *Nihonshoki* and the *Kojiki* imply that aristocratic mansions and palaces came into existence during the fifth century and that their style was a combination of traditional Japanese residential traditions and those of the Korean peninsula.

The Demon's Castle

The hillside fortresses and lookout settlements prevalent in coastal Kibi in Yayoi times did not disappear but took on a stronger and more significant role within the community. They followed a definite original Korean pattern with probable later Puyo Kayan, and then north Korean additions.

High on the hills overlooking the Ashimori and Takahashi river deltas rise the enormous walls of the legendary Demon's Castle of Kibi. Four hundred metres above sea level on Mt Kijo, the walls stretch 2.5 kilometres and virtually encircle the summit; the castle area is almost equal to that of the old City of London. This could be the 'palace at Ashimori' of Princess Kuro's father, sovereign of Kibi, where the *Nihonshoki* suggests the Yamato 'Emperor' Ojin 'removed his dwelling'. In the *Kojiki* it is the 'Emperor' Nintoku.

The first serious archaeological survey of the

25. A view from the walls of the Demon's Castle, central Kibi, looking eastwards towards Yamato. Equally fine views to the west are to be had from this seemingly impregnable fortress. It was probably designed as a retreat position and could house several thousand soldiers for many months. There are paddy fields in the small valleys behind the fortress. The flood gate system is ancient north Korean in style. This castle was said to be the home of the Ura or demon, who was finally routed by Kibitsu Hiko. The Ura is obviously a folk allusion for 'Koreans' or Puyo/Kayan/Kibi people finally defeated by Yamato.

ruins began in 1970 under the auspices of the Okayama Prefectural Museum. This suggested that the structure may have been built by Korean immigrants and a Korean archaeologist, Jin Hui Lee, was one of a group of experts who then visited the castle. He was particularly interested in the floodgate design which he described as very similar to the systems used in north Korean hilltop castles to supply water to the garrison. The walls, too, are similar to Korean examples and extend for about 2.5 kilometres on the southern face of the summit. To the north other traces of walls have been found, guarding the crests of valleys.

A survey of the castle in 1977 produced evidence that the area had been inhabited since the Jomon era. The castle itself was probably first constructed when the kings of Kibi fought with Yamato between the fourth and sixth centuries.

Later additions were made in the seventh century following a nationwide imperial edict requiring provincial fortifications against the threat of Korean attacks.

The castle is ideally sited; the southern walls command a 180 degree view overlooking the seaways to Kibi from the east and west. The plains below, now dotted with tumuli, can be seen clearly in every direction. The defenders had a perfect view of any force invading from east or west, by land or sea, while the steep cliffs crowned by the walls provided an almost impenetrable barrier. Behind the fortifications at a height of about 300 metres is a large area of well-irrigated paddy. This farmland would have been capable of feeding a large garrison for a considerable period.

Recently discovered foundation stones in the centre of the fortification are believed to be those of storehouses, which must have been large enough to provision several thousand soldiers for a year. Other remains of storehouses and gatehouses have been discovered within the castle complex as the survey progresses. One of the most immediate problems with the survey of the castle site is its current inaccessibility from roads and major urban areas. The 1977 study lasted two months and included a visit to Korea with a budget of only 8.5 million Yen contributed by the provincial media; it was supervised by thirteen local experts. The otherwise excellent archaeological report published in 1977 stresses the seventh century origins of the castle but makes little reference to earlier inhabitation. One can only speculate whether the project would be better funded and understood if it were not for some of the prevailing xenophobia about Korean influence upon Japan in the early centuries.

The Demon Dies

One of the best sources of clues in piecing together this sort of historical puzzle is usually local folklore. The Kibi area is rich in such tales and herein may lie the story of the end of one of the periods of Kibi power. People brought up in Kibi often relate the fable of Prince Kibitsu and his fight with the demon. The story is inscribed in the official annals as part of the origin of the beautiful Kibitsu Shrine on the side of Mt. Naka. These chapters known as the *Kibitsu-Miya-no-Engi* were copied from an earlier account during the Edo period. The *Kibi-Miya-no-Engi* is a little different from some other versions but a general theme runs through them all.

During the reign of the Yamato King Suinin (in some books, Sujin, with date of death, cycle adjusted, perhaps AD 258 or 318), a demon god flew to Kibi from a far away country. He was said to be a prince of Paekche (the Korean kingdom founded by the Puyo) and his name was Ura—but he was also known as Kibi-no-Kaja (the Kibi demon from Kaya?). His eyes were abnormally large and shone like those of a wild animal; his hair was flame-red and he stood fourteen feet high. Like many demons, he was incredibly strong and vicious. At first he built his residence at Niiyama; nearby on Mt Kijo he built a castle. He robbed the ships which carried tribute from the western lands to the Yamato court and terrorized women and children. People were terrified of him and called the castle *Ki-no-jo*: 'the Demon's Castle'. Finally, the people of Kibi petitioned the king in Yamato for help. The Yamato court heard this plea and sent a general to subdue the demon. The fight was long and furious but in the end the Yamato general retreated in disarray. Hearing of this defeat, the king then dispatched the famous warrior, Prince Isaseri-hiko-no-Mikoto (later named Prince Kibitsu) with a large army and navy. The prince entered Kibi and encamped his force near Mt Naka. The site he chose was at Kataokayama (site of the Joto ruins); there he built a stone fortification and prepared for battle. Strange stones are still to be seen there, lying within the precincts of Tatetsuki Shrine, laid in circles, and are of great significance in the study of early religious rites, and the rock cult of the Puyo.

Prince Isaseri-hiko attacked the demon but found progress very difficult because of supernatural forces. The demon seemed to be able to harness thunder and lightning to strike the prince's army, and when Isaseri-hiko brought up his archers, they found that their arrows were knocked out of the sky by those of the demon; the arrows fell into the sea and at Oishimura is a small shrine called Yagui dedicated to them; it consists of six enormous rocks with strange markings purporting to have been made by the arrows. Only when Prince Isaseri put two arrows in his bow and fired them simultaneously did he manage to wound the demon in the left eye. Blood spurted like water out of the eye into the Chisuigawa ('blood water') River which flows into the Ashimori River, directly below the great castle ruins. The demon was transformed into a pheasant and sought refuge in the mountains while the prince, in his turn, changed into a hawk and gave chase. As the pheasant was about to be caught by him he again changed his guise to that of a carp and dived into a river. Prince Isaseri-hiko then became a cormorant, swooped, grabbed the carp in his beak, and killed it. In death the carp returned to the form of the demon. To signal his victory over the demon, the prince took part of his name from Kibi-no-Kaja (the demon) and was known from then on, in the histories, as Prince Kibitsu-Hiko-no-Mikoto.

After the victory the prince cut off the demon's head and impaled it on a bamboo pole which was publicly displayed at Koube in eastern Kibi, a point near to Yamato, where a ruin still exists. Many years later the head still kept muttering, so Prince Kibitsu instructed his retainer, Inukai-

26. The *kamaden* (kitchen) at the Kibitsu Shrine. The sound and pitch of the steam from the rice cooking pot is still used in religious divination. The iron rice pot was made by the iron casters of Azo, who lived on the mountain near the Demon's Castle. The Ura or demon is reputed to have presented the rice pot along with his wife to Kibitsu Hiko. The demon's head is said to be buried underneath the *Kamadan*. The female shrine attendants have always, traditionally, come from Azo and carry that patronym. The head priests at Kibitsu Shrine until very recently all carried the family name Kaya.

no-Takeru, to feed the head to his dog, but the skull continued to mutter. Finally it was brought back to Prince Kibitsu's headquarters at Mt Naka and buried under the kitchens in the precincts of the great shrine which had been erected to celebrate the victory. The muttering nevertheless went on for a further thirteen years, until one night in a dream, the spirit of the demon appeared to Prince Kibitsu and told him to take the Demon's wife, Azo-Hime, and appoint her a shrine attendant to work in the kitchens. He also told Prince Kibitsu that fortunes could be told by the pitch of the note coming from the rice pot as it bubbled. He said that Prince Kibitsu should become a priest and use the demon's spirit to control the first four aristocratic ranks. Thereupon the kitchen became a sacred site known today as the *kamaden*—a place of prayer for the demon's spirit. This is the origin of the Kamanari-shinji rituals and the noise of the rice cooker is still used today for religious divination. The author has witnessed this rite and heard the 'divine' sounds.

In the time of the kings Suinin and Sujin, it would have been very difficult to raise an army sufficiently equipped to withstand the rigours of a long journey by land to attack a distant state. As discussed in Chapter II, the communities of those times were only just emerging from a tribal society and becoming clan states ruled by chieftains. The legend undoubtedly stems from a more recent period, but because of the difficulty of producing a credible historical document in the eighth century, many of the stories told by Hieda-no-Are were slotted in wherever they seemed to help the narrative, rather than chronologically.

My own view is that Kibitsu-Hiko has his rightful place in the late fourth century.

Perhaps the most unusual feature of the Tatetsuki Shrine complex and the nearby Obosan cemetery, where the house-topped *haniwa* was found, is a triangular-shaped stone about 1.75 metres in circumference which was discovered buried near the great rocks. The stone, called *kameishi* ('turtle stone') is carved with weird intertwined lines and whirls. Archaeological opinion is that the stone is an omphalos or the naval of the Kibi kingdom. Similar stones have been found elsewhere in western Japan, but the Tatetsuki example is unique. It is quite likely that the placement of this stone at Tatetsuki was divined by Puyo shaman geomancers. Early in 1998, the ruins of a port system were also discovered near the Tatetsuki ruins, adding support to my premise that Kibi and the Demon's Castle were attacked also from the sea. It is interesting to note that, along a straight line from Tatetsuki to the castle, are many shrines dedicated to events in the story of Kibitsu-Hiko and his battle with the demon. If this line is continued it whould eventually cross the Sea of Japan and end at the Sungari River delta in Manchuria, from whence the Puyo horse riders started their Korean conquests. All along this line, Shinto shrines are to be found. Some experts believe that the stones at Tatetsuki and those at Yagui Shrine, near the Chisui River, are the remnants of a star geomancy arranged around central monoliths, now missing.

I believe that the shrines along the line mark the battle phases of the Puyo/Kayan conquest of Kibi, and that the ultimate destination was

27. The Tatetsuki ruins where the *kameishi* (turtle) omphalos stone and numerous tombs were discovered; probably the site of the Kayan/Puyo/Kayan landings. Probably late fourth century AD. Tatetsuki, meaning 'shield shape' is a hilltop with an unusual and perhaps unique stone circle about ten metres in diameter. Some of these enormous stones have been worked into bizarre shapes, some resembling furniture (a couch, an armchair and stool). Experts believe that the remnants represent a six-pointed star geomancy arranged around a central monolith. Two burials were found, one with the floor painted in cinnabar, *magatama* (beads shaped like 'bear claws') and an iron sword. It is possible that the huge stones were also painted with cinnabar which was believed to be the elixir of everlasting life. The remains of a drainage system also suggest that the area was not only used for burials, but was probably a fortress.

28. The *kameishi* (turtle stone) or omphalos discovered at the Tatetsuki ruins in central Kibi. This mysterious stone is carved with linked wavy lines and eyes which remind one of a turtle. The decoration is related to the Chokkomon design found in both Kyushu and other parts of Kibi. The stone and its positioning suggests that it represents the central location point in Kibi. Many shrines lie along a line from where this stone was buried to the Demon's Castle. These shrines originally commemorated battles between the invading forces. The graves at Tatetsuki are probably those of important military figures or chieftains.

Photo: David Bauer

29. Korean shamanistic vestiges in the form of enormous dolmen, at the Joto ruins, Obosan (King's Cemetery), third–fourth century AD. Kibi is well endowed with such monoliths which are believed to be vestiges of the Korean shamanistic rock cult imported from Kaya. Rocks were thought to contain *kami* (spirits or gods) and thus were venerated. Small shrines are almost always placed nearby.

Kinojo, the Demon's Castle, which was attacked twice: once by the Puyo and, two centuries later, by the Yamato unification league. It is no coincidence that the river that winds down from the Demon's Castle through these sites to the ancient estuary and recently discovered port ruins is called Chisui—the River of Blood.

One of the greatest problems with the *Nihonshoki* (AD 720) is that when Ono Yasumaro was commissioned to write it, he used the Chinese system of dates in cycles of sixty years starting with Year One at 660 BC. This gave him more years than he had material to fill, so he used not only his own and the empress's imagination, but also plucked out and included whole chunks of Chinese and Korean history to suit his convenience. Some tales were stretched and some characters split into different parts while the reigns of many early kings were extended to pad out

the chronicle.

The eighth century was a period of great Yamato nationalism and identity; just as the historians saw little wrong with copying Chinese and Korean history to suit their own purposes, they also had no conscience about turning a Kibi hero into a Yamato figure and using his exploits to bolster their own prestige. This is what happened with Prince Kibitsu. In the folk story he arrived in Kibi known as Prince Isaseri-Hiko-no-Mikoto and after victory took part of his enemy's name: Kibi-no-Kaja. Both Prince Kibitsu and Kibi-no-Kaja were, I feel sure, princes from the Korean peninsula and became either the rulers or military governors of Kibi – one of the early federated Wa states controlled from Kaya in southern Korea. The fact that even Japanese archaeologists have admitted that the walls of the Demon's Castle on Mt Kijo are Korean in style would tend to support the thesis that part of the story dealing with the metamorphosis of the demon and Prince Kibitsu was lifted from the Korean legend about Chumong, the founder of the kingdom of Koguryo, ancestral home of the Puyo horse riders. The most logical date for Prince Kibitsu would be the latter part of the reign of King Nintoku (late fourth century) and it is likely that he came as governor of Kibi after the Puyo people had conquered the original Kayan kingdom, extended their territory into Wa and reformed the federation of Wa states. The Puyo people, as mentioned before, originated in what is now known as Manchuria. They were fine horsemen and roamed southward, where they became the founders and rulers of Paekche. As they moved on further south they took with them a large number of slaves; these they brought to Wa together with their horses, and it would have been comparatively easy to subdue the Wa people, which they did, rapidly, from Kaya to Kyushu and on to the east.

As this new wave of Puyo/Kayan colonists moved up the Inland Sea, they established their hilltop fortresses as they went. Possibly the only real obstacle they encountered was at Kibi, where they met with a resistance developed by years of earlier Kayan immigration. Kibi's navy was renowned, and, together with its land forces, put up a stern fight against the new Puyo/Kayan people before being finally overwhelmed.

The dating of the two colossal tumuli in Kibi and the even larger ones in Yamato corresponds with the period when Korean historians believe that the Puyo overran Kaya. Professor Gari Ledyard, of Columbia University, believes that the Puyo/Kayan forces attacked Japan and conquered it in AD 369—thirty years before the death of Emperor Nintoku.

We should remember that Emperor Nintoku, or King San as he was known by the Chinese, was one of the mysterious 'five kings of Wa' referred to earlier. After the Puyo/Kayan cavalry had defeated Kibi, they probably built or re-built the enormous castle on Mt Kijo with their imported slave labour. Noting the local reverence for tumuli, they would have constructed their tumuli to dimensions never seen before. This would account for the sudden development of the tombs described in Chapter 4. Reference to the chart on page 58 underlines my conjecture that a powerful external influence was responsible for the rapid appearance and disappearance

Photo: David Bauer

30. Monolithic rocks, some moved into place by the Kayan/Puyo invaders to form a burial site; third–fourth century AD. This site is still used today as a Shinto shrine. The practice of rock worship shares many characteristics with similar practices in Korea. The area exudes an aura of fear and the sensation that something quite dreadful must have happened here. Evidence of a tomb is clear. The forces necessary to have moved some of these rocks must have been enormous and involved the labour of thousands of people.

of such huge slave-built edifices. That two enormous tumuli lie in the shadow of Mt Kijo on the plains beneath the castle walls is added confirmation of the theory and, should this be valid, it is equally reasonable to suppose that Prince Kibitsu, an early Puyo/Kayan military governor of Kibi, may be one of the occupants of one of the two great Kibi tumuli.

Over the past years I have pondered whether it was at Kibi that the idea of big tumuli originated, and whether the first was the 270 metre long Sakuzan followed by the 350 metre Tsukuryama about two kilometres away. The sizes and lengths of the tombs become larger as we move eastward, ending with the vast tomb of Nintoku in Yamato which occupies 32 hectares and is over 800 metres in length. The construction of tombs the size of Nintoku's would have taken about eighteen years, while the Kibi pair would have taken at least ten years each, the castle possibly longer. Many thousands of labourers would have been employed on each project. The colonists therefore must have settled for some time in Kibi before moving eastwards to attack Yamato. This would have been a combined naval and cavalry operation, with the indigenous Kibi people also committed to the cause. The Yamato tombs of Kings Ojin, Nintoku and Ritchu are, if this Puyo theory holds, the final resting places of dynastic Puyo/Kayan conquerors who established themselves as kings. Almost all Japanese historians and archaeologists agree that the real origins of the Japanese imperial lineage lie in the fifth century. It is not difficult now to understand why the Imperial Household Agency is reluctant to open these larger tombs for archaeological inspection.

My argument does not militate against my other theory on the usurpation of the throne by Prince Hoshikawa and his Kibi mother after King Yuryaku's death. After the conquest of Yamato, the Korean horsemen and raiders drove even further eastwards, to areas near Sendai, encountering stiff opposition all the way. There are probably more tumuli of the mounted nobility in the Kanto plain area, near Tokyo, than anywhere else, pointing to long and protracted fighting against primitive but strong pockets of resistance. As in any empire won by conquest, the Puyo/Kayan/Yamato kings found that the further their territories extended, the more difficult they were to control. With commitments from Kibi in the west to their colonial wars in the east, the new rulers chose Yamato as a base, utilizing trusted generals for their eastern expeditions. King Yuryaku, the fifth or sixth of his dynasty, covered his Kibi flank by marrying the wife of one of the kings of Kibi, Princess Waka, who bore him two sons. One of these, as we have seen, Prince Hoshikawa, declared civil war and seized the throne briefly upon his father's death, but was finally ousted by the Yamato nobles who presumably recalled their eastern armies to deal with this threat. If we return to the folk tale of Prince Kibitsu and the demon, we can see how and why Kibi really fell. Prince Isaseri Hiko-no-Mikoto, the great warrior sent by the Yamato king to conquer the demon, was, in all probability, a general sent by Yuryaku's ultimate heir, King Seinei, to punish and dispossess the princes of upper Kibi of their mountain domains, centered on the Demon's Castle on Mt Kijo. This final dispossession was a bloody affair, with decisive battles, before the Kibi forces retreated into the castle, taking place along the Chisuigawa at the foot of Mt Kijo. In the end, the Kibi forces were probably starved into surrender.

The folk tale is a hodgepodge of many stories and Prince Kibitsu was a convenient figurehead for the self-glorification of the later eighth century 'imperial' family. By the time of the final destruction of the castle, Prince Kibitsu must have been long in his grave. It was not in the interests of the historians and court of the eighth century to clarify the means and manner of their increased sophistication, so references to an eastward Puyo/Kayan invasion were suppressed and the facts ignored. In their stead, it is simply recorded that an infusion of skilled craftsmen and artists from China and Korea took place at the request of the native Yamato kings. This is about as plausible as suggesting that an eighteenth century Australian aboriginal chieftain personally and successfully requested the King of England to send cloth manufacturers and tailors to clothe his people.

The Puyo and Kaya People in Kibi

While Kibi was temporarily subjugated, the aristocracy of Yamato set out to create order out of chaos, only to find themselves plagued with internal disagreements—a not uncommon misfortune for oriental monarchies. Examination of the genealogical table of Yamato kings reveals that between the last of the five 'kings of Wa' Yuryaku (Bu) who died in AD 479, and the accession of Kimmei in AD 540, seven kings ruled the country, with one of these kings, Keitai, reigning for twenty-four years.

It is therefore clear that the descendants of some of the 'five kings of Wa' were constantly involved in an internecine struggle; not until the accession of Kemmei in AD 540 was royal authority consolidated. The Japanese nation had arrived. This brought an end to the continual political manoeuvering and treachery which characterized the ancient tribal clan communities. The formation of a formal hereditary monarchy with a Chinese/Korean style of centralized government resulted in rapid cultural advancement; the Buddhist religion in its Chinese form began to gain adherents; a class system devel-

oped, with the aristocracy in control, and for the first time a Japanese cultural identity began to blossom.

During the late fifth and early sixth centuries, the Puyo/Kayan invaders consolidated their hold over the old clan chieftains of 'Wa' and there was regular contact with the Korean peninsula. Paekche was continually involved in skirmishes with the neighbouring kingdom of Silla, and frequently called upon its Puyo/Kayan allies in Wa for support. At one point Ki-no-Oiwa, the son of Ki-no-Oyumi, the general who had been sent by King Yuryaku to attack Silla, instigated a revolt against Wa in Kaya. He attempted to establish an independent kingdom in Korea for himself and even succeeded in building a capital, which he called Taisanjo. In the tradition of his seafaring ancestors from the province of Ki, he proceeded to intercept convoys sailing between Paekche and Wa. This could not last, and in AD 487 the Paekche army attacked his forces and put them to flight. From the account of his revolt we can see clearly that the old Wa hegemony was no longer concentrated in Kaya. The power centre was now firmly established in Yamato, and the difficulty of controlling distant territory was becoming very pronounced.

From the Yayoi period through the fourth, fifth and sixth centuries, most of Japan was primarily controlled by Koreans. The Kaya and later the Puyo/Kayan invaders brought with them a language and government replacing many of the primitive tribal forms of rule. The newcomers arrived with ranks and titles which they continued to use; local clan chieftains who acknowledged the new court were similarly ennobled and privileged. The language used at court was probably that of the new people—Altaic—and with usage became intermixed with the local tongue.

Both ancient and modern Japanese historians are fond of using the term 'naturalized' when describing the newcomers, thereby suggesting that they became adopted citizens in a Japanese sense. This is illogical and confusing, for the contrary was most likely the case. The Puyo/Kayan people slowly admitted to citizenship those local people who conformed to their wishes and ideals, for the power to confer citizenship was a Puyo prerogative. The first Puyo/Kayan people arrived as conquerors, *not* by osmotic absorption as today's Japanese would prefer to believe.

The old clans were reformed into patrilineal groups known as *uji*, a term brought by the Puyo from their ancestral land in Manchuria. Clans acknowledged by the court were given territorial names which also had sub-divisions. For example, in Kibi-Shimotsumichi and Kibi-Kamitsumichi, the leaders of the clans were termed *Omi*, and this title implied a close relationship with the central court. A clan was divided into numerous smaller septs following the Paekche (Puyo) pattern of occupation (*pu*). The local corruption of the term *pu* was *be* meaning a form of guild, headed by skilled technicians from Paekche and later Koguryo. Today the same ideogram now pronounced *bu* is in common use; i.e., *Bucho* – 'section chief or manager'. The paramount ruler of each district was called the *Kuni-no-Miyatsuko*. In some areas the Uji served as leaders. In Kibi, the Kuni-no-Miyatsuko were

powerful independent figures, provincial governors, who later had authority to levy taxes. Such governors often became despots and had to be suppressed. Examples were seen in the mid-fifth century case of Sakitsuya's contempt for King Yuryaku and the later rebellion of the Omi of upper Kibi who were dispossessed of their lands by King Seinei (r. AD 480–484).

Local Omi were expected to vow fealty to the central authority—the sovereign—through the lending of fighting men and tradesmen such as potters, cooks, weavers and embroiderers. A further example of this is the story of Sakitsuya, the *Omi* of Kibi-by-the-Sea (Shimotsumichi), and the officer of the archers' *be*, O-sora. The *be* in which O-sora served was on duty at the central court and was recalled by Sakitsuya, who had probably quarrelled with the central authority; this story from the *Nihonshoki* shows how some *Omi* disputed the power of the Yamato authority.

In Kibi, perhaps more than elsewhere in Japan, we can find very clear evidence of the vast waves of immigrants who came in the fourth and fifth centuries and settled. These people brought with them new skills which they practiced locally. As in Korea, they separated into family groups or *be* in areas suitable to their particular craft. Some of the iron workers, for example, settled in the hills near Mt Kijo at Niiyama (curiously, the same place where the Ura, demon of Kibi, lived) close to the source of the Chisuigawa. The name of their *be* guild was the Azobe; their main patronym was Lin, which was later corrupted to the Japanese pronunciation of the ideogram—Hayashi. The Lin or Hayashi family lived and worked in Niiyama until the fourteenth century when they moved to the plains near Ashimori. Their new village was called Azo and flanked the banks of the Chisuigawa River, rich in iron sands. It still exists, divided into East Azo and West Azo, and almost every family still bears the name Hayashi. The early Lin ironworkers were casters rather than forgers, making agricultural equipment, cooking vessels, large nails used in temple construction and temple bells. In the Edo period there were nine iron foundries working but today only one survives, on the evidence of a recent visit.

Traditionally, the Azobe have made the great cooking cauldrons (*Kama*) at Kibitsu Shrine (the first, presented by the Ura or demon together with his wife Azo-hime); their bells became national treasures and their nails also held together the great Todaiji Temple at Nara.

In Kibi, some of the settlers came from Paekche and many from Kaya, where the original branch states of Wa were controlled. Korean chronicles tell of the Puyo people's conquest of Kaya and Professor Ledyard maintains that the equestrian hordes then moved with their retainers across to the Japanese archipelago. The newcomers, as mentioned, probably had little trouble in toppling the local chieftains in Kyushu and far western Honshu, but ran into severe opposition from the Kibi chieftains, who were well known for their military and naval prowess, and because of their continued mercantile contact with the Korean mainland, they were more sophisticated than most of the western clans. After finally defeating Kibi, the Puyo/Kayan invaders settled for some time and set up their leader as king of all they conquered to the west, includ-

ing most of Kibi. Their slaves settled too, and gathered into guilds. At this time additional work on the strategic castle on Mt Kijo began, with the *be* settled in its shadow. The construction of the castle, involving the transport and positioning of enormous rocks, made an ideal project to engage the extensive labour force at the disposal of the colonists; similar but much smaller hilltop castles are found all along the Inland Sea and in northern Kyushu – they were probably constructed at about the same time. The original fort was most probably located close to the Azobe (iron workers) on Mt Niiyama overlooking the Ashimori River. They then prepared for the final onslaught on the clans of Yamato.

Between the Takahashi and Asahi rivers on either side of the smaller Ashimori River, which runs between them for a stretch of some twenty kilometres, one can still find numerous villages with the predominant family name either of Hata or Kaya. *Hata* (*pada*) in Korean means 'the sea', whereas in Japanese it means 'weaver'; it was presumably used to describe people who came from afar by sea, while the Kaya obviously took the name of their homeland. The Hata tribe may have been slaves from southern Paekche captured by the Puyo as they swept south into Kaya. The Hata became a weavers' guild known as the Hata-*be* or Hata-*hito* and were later involved in silk cultivation and iron smelting; they lived in eastern and central Kibi particularly around the modern town of Ashimori and Soja City.

The first known Buddhist temple in Kibi was vast and was erected at a village called Hata, now part of Soja City, near Kurashiki City in c. 630 AD. It was set by the side of a hill in a most picturesque setting and called Hata-bara. The 3.6 square metre foundation stone of the central pagoda, and evidence of other buildings can still be seen; tiles manufactured nearby date from the late sixth century AD. These are stylistically different from any other tiles found in Japan but closely resemble Paekche originals found among Puyo ruins in south-west Korea.

The patronym Kaya occurs frequently in the *Nihonshoki*, one of the earliest references being in the tale of Princess Kuro and King Ojin. When the king divided Kibi among the family of Mitomo-Wake, Princess Kuro's father, Princess Kuro was granted the district of the Hattori-be (Hata-be), now known as Kaya-gun and according to the *Nihonshoki*, it is here that Ojin's and Kuro's descendants settled. The princess's brother was granted Kibi-Kamitsumichi (eastern Kibi) and was chronicled as the ancestor of the Omi of Kaya. If the *Nihonshoki* is to be believed then, since Mitomo-Wake was Prince Kibitsu-hiko's son, and his son Nakatsuhiko the ancestor of the 0mi of Kaya, logically so was Prince Kibitsu. This might corroborate my contention that Prince Kibitsu was a Korean prince and an early ruler of Kibi, and maybe the Puyo/Kayan King Shi of Wa.

The Omi of Kaya reappear later during the Nara period (AD 710–784), being involved with the collection of taxes in Bitchu province in central Kibi. The Kaya-be also seem to have settled in Kibi in a similar pattern to that of the Hata. From the north-east of Soja City through to northwest Okayama City, the old Kaya name is still found; in Kaya-gun there is a village called Hattori-go with a temple called Kaya-no-Kaya-Dera and some families called Kara (Kaya), while north of Ashimori is a hamlet called Kaya Mura. In Okayama City itself can be found the Nishi (west) Kara (Kaya) River and the Kara (Kaya) river market, and at Kayano in Okayama City there is a mountain peak called Karako (Kayako) Toge. Perhaps the most significant use of the name of Kaya is at the great Kibitsu Shrine where the chief priests, until very recently, consistently bore Kaya as their family name.

Achi-no-Omi, Prince of Han

One of the most puzzling Kibi-related characters to appear in both the early chronicles is Prince Achi who was alleged by both to be the descendant of the Chinese emperor of Han, Ling-ti (reigned AD 160–190). The *Nihonshoki* states that in the fifteenth year of the reign of the King Ojin, which corresponds to AD 411 (adjusted for the sixty year cycle), Prince Achi and his son Tsuga-no-Omi emigrated to Japan accompanied by a large group from seventeen districts in Paekche. The *Kojiki* refers to Prince Achi in a slightly different context and explains that King Kunch'ogo of Paekche presented a stallion, a mare, a miraculous 'cross-sword' and a mirror to the King of Japan. These gifts, together with a blacksmith and a weaver from the Chinese kingdom of 'Go', which had close relations with Paekche, were brought to Japan by Prince Achi. According to the *Kojiki*, Prince Achi was the ancestor of the Achiki-no-Fumihito but the *Nihonshoki* made him the forefather of the Aya-Atabe of Yamato. There is a discrepancy between the Korean dating of King Kunch'ogo and the

Japanese version. According to the Koreans, Kunch'ogo reigned from AD 346 to 379, corresponding with the reign of King Nintoku as dated by both the Nihonshoki and Kojiki. Given the acknowledged two-cycle discrepancy in the Japanese histories, it seems preferable to accept the Korean dates.

A cross-sword with an inscription and date is kept at the Isonokami Shrine in Nara prefecture. The recently deciphered gold-inlaid inscription reads as follows:

"This seven branch sword was made of finely wrought iron on the sixteenth day of the fourth month of Tai-ho. It has a miraculous power to put the enemy to rout. I shall present it to the king. Made by........(name indecipherable). Never has there been such a sword. The King of Paekche and his son, who owe their lives to the august Chin, had this sword made for King 'Shi' of Wa with the hope that it be transmitted in posterity."

The year of Tai-ho has been almost positively identified as AD 369—the date when Professor Ledyard believes the Puyo/Kayan invaders moved on to the archipelago.

Japanese academics have been greatly excited by the translation of the inscription and have gone to great lengths to interpret the manner in which the sword was presented from the King of Paekche to the King of Wa. The debate is one of nuance: whether the sword was 'bestowed' or 'offered up'. Naturally the Japanese prefer 'offered up', its implication being that Paekche was a vassal state of Wa. This might well have been the case but my view is that the debate surrounding the sword owes more to the fierce national-

ism and mutual hatred that constantly colours discussion of the Japan-Korea historical connection. The manner of presentation is a red herring. More to the point is the correct interpretation of Wa. The sword was probably given in tribute to the Puyo conqueror of Wa (at that stage he had only reached Kaya), prior to his assault on the Wa branch-states on the Japanese archipelago.

The *Kojiki* refers to another miraculous cross-sword in its chapter on the first King Jimmu (660-585 BC). The heavenly deities are said to have presented Jimmu with a cross-sword before his final conquest of the eastern provinces. The Kojiki says that 'This sword dwells in the Temple of the deity of Isonokami'. In the part of the *Nihonshoki* dealing with the Queen Regent Jingu-Kogo (AD 201-269) in AD 251 can be found a precise account of the kings of Paekche, father and son, making representation to Wa. 'They beat their foreheads on the ground . . . the immense bounty of the honourable country . . . more weighty than heaven and earth . . . the sage sovereign dwells above, illustrious as the sun and moon; thy servants now dwell below . . . never showing double hearts'. In the following year they 'presented a seven-branch sword and seven-little-one-mirror with various other objects of great value'.

Given the cyclical error in dating, the adjusted dates of AD 371 and 372 coincide neatly with the AD 369 on the sword at Isonokami Shrine. Paradoxically both early histories state that the Queen Regent Jingu-Kogo attacked and conquered Korea – a curious but predictable inversion of the truth. I believe that the Jimmu cross-

31. The seven-branched iron sword with a 48 character inscription inlaid in gold, dated AD 369. Presented to the King of Wa by the ruler of Paekche. Possibly part of the original Japanese (Puyo) imperial regalia until the inscription was found to contradict later eighth century AD xenophobia. The sword is kept within the sacred precincts of the Isonokami Shrine in Yamato. The Puyo National Museum in Korea has a replica exhibited near its entrance. The sword measures 74.5 cm. The seven branches represent the seven heavens in shamanistic symbolism. The seven branches can also be found on gold crowns excavated in both Korea and Japan.

sword, the Jingu-Kogo seven-branch sword, the Achi-no-Omi cross-sword and the seven branch sword with the gold inlaid inscription in the Isonokami Shrine are one and the same. The Jingu-Kogo chapters on AD 371 and AD 372 (dates cycle adjusted) indicate a strong possibility that, at the time of the compilation of the *Nihonshoki* and *Kojiki* in the early eighth century, the inscription on the sword was still visible and that Hieda-no-Are, Ono-Yasumaro and the court were all aware that it was the first king's sword, which would explain the reference to it in the first King Jimmu section of the Kojiki. The compilers' dissatisfaction with the inscription was then, as now, caused by the implications of the manner in which the weapon was either 'offered up' or 'bestowed'. In order to emphasize their preference for the depiction of Paekche as subservient to Wa throughout history, they deliberately shuffled the cycles and stressed the Paekche kings' submissive attitude in 371 and sword presentation in 372. I am also convinced that the gift of the cross-sword, 'large mirror' and horses was a presentation from King Kunch'ogo delivered to King Shi, who brought them to Japan after they had been delivered by Achi-no-Omi in Kaya. It is obvious from the expression 'put the enemy to rout' that the recipient was a warrior, about to embark for war. The Puyo were horsemen, so the gift of a breeding pair was particularly significant; after all, King Kunch'ogo would have known that King Shi was embarking for Japan where horses were rare. The sword and mirror were carried to Kibi and would have rested there before the final subjugation of Yamato, and were later enshrined.

King Shi of Wa was almost certainly the first king of the new Puyo/Kayan dynasty and his tomb may be one of the two colossal tumuli in Kibi. My conclusion is that he died before the final defeat of Yamato which was completed by his descendants. The seven-branch sword and the seven-little-one-mirror were probably the original imperial regalia in use until the eighth century when historians, under imperial influence, began to distort the records. It is not unreasonable to assume that Prince Achi travelled to Japan with the commanding general as a senior advisor in charge of the artisans from 'seventeen of his home districts'. These came from the original Kaya and Hata clans; they settled and worked in Kibi just as their descendants moved on to Yamato and settled there after its defeat. It is unlikely that Prince Achi was a descendant of Emperor Ling-ti of the Chinese Han dynasty. I feel that it is most likely that this deliberate confusion arose through the similarity of names between the Chinese dynasty and the separate Han tribes of south Korea in Kaya. The eighth century Japanese court would have been delighted to recount and claim that a Chinese rather than Korean imperial prince had chosen to immigrate to Japan. The ideogram used to write the Korean word Aya, the name of one of the most powerful tribes in Kaya, can also be read as Han. Prince Achi, according to the *Nihonshoki*, was the forerunner of the Atahe of the Aya of Yamato. The Aya emigrants were associated with the Hata and Kaya, who were iron casters, weavers and silk producers. Prince Achi's connection with textiles is emphasised in both the early histories; in one account he is described as having been sent by the court with his son to 'Kure', probably in China, to recruit seamstresses.

In modern Kurashiki City, there are numerous places named Achi. The old name for the town itself was Achi and a shrine dedicated to Achi-no-Omi is to be found on Mt Tsurugata overlooking the canal and museum area. In ancient times, numerous bays around Kojima took the name Achi, although none remain with that name now, possibly because of land reclamation. The reclaimed land around Kurashiki was once called Achi-gata which gives some credence to this theory. There is no concrete evidence that Prince Achi ever lived in Kibi although the possibility must exist; his reputed residence in Yamato is called Hinoki-Sumi where there is a shrine dedicated to him called Omi Ashi (Prince's Legs). In Nishi-Achi in Kurashiki is another shrine, called Achi-Nyojin, famed for its ability to assuage leg pains through prayer. Achi-Nyojin is also connected with the textile industry and is probably a branch of the Omi-Ashi Shrine at Hinoki-Sumi, the headquarters of the Aya of Yamato. At some time, in the eighth century, the Yamato Aya split up into over sixty groups and settled in distant parts of Japan. One of these groups may have come and settled in Kurashiki, erecting a shrine to their guardian spirit. The ninth century *Wamyosho* records that the Yamato Aya dominated the community wherever they settled. Their patronyms in the Kurashiki area today are Kaya, Inukai and Hirata. In Nishi-Achi, in Kurashiki, there was a local village headman called Kaya who built a temple there called Teirinji; there is also a temple of this name close to the Omi-Ashi Shrine in

Yamato. At the Kurashiki Nishi-Achi Teirinji is a stone five-ringed pagoda called Achi-Maro-Sama. At one time there was a group of villages in Kurashiki called Higashi-Achi-Go, one of which was called Sugo and another Masu, now known as Hirata. Hirata is believed to be one of the oldest reclaimed areas in Kibi. There are still families named Hirata living in the village in beautiful old farm houses, who are probably the descendants of the Yamato Aya who moved to the area in the eighth century.

The name of Inukai has already been referred to in the story of the demon and Prince Kibitsu; it was Inukai-no-Takeru who was instructed by his master to feed the Demon's head to his dog. The descendants of Inukai-no-Takeru still live near Kibitsu Shrine and their most famous representative in modern times was Tsuyoshi Inukai, the prime minister of Japan, whose assassination in 1932 led to the political upheaval culminating in Japan's involvement in World War II.

Yamato Centralizes on Kibi

The Omi of Kibi in the sixth century appear to have held great power even after the failed coup d'état of Prince Hoshikawa and his mother, Princess Waka of Kibi, in Yamato. This is evidenced by the many huge tumuli with later style horizontal burial chambers found in the area where the Omi lived. In an historical document compiled by the Yamato Central Government there is an account of their establishment of miyake, these were rice fields and granaries belonging to and producing tax for the imperial estate; they were controlled directly by the Yamato court and placed in the charge of officials called Miyake Obito. The farmers who cultivated the imperial land were termed tabe and their overseers tabe-no-Muraji. From the document we cannot be sure when the system of miyake was introduced but it is clear that they were established first in areas of political sensitivity. The Nihonshoki tells us that in the reign of Emperor Ankan in AD 535, miyake were established in Kibi gokoku. Gokoku implies that this was at the greatest distance from Yamato. Obviously Yamato was extremely concerned about the strength of Kibi based on its strategic position on the Inland Sea and its great iron industry. These two factors were the main reasons for Yamato tightening its grip on Kibi.

In AD 556 the Emperor Kimmei sent two powerful ministers from Yamato to Kibi, named Soga-no-Iname-no-Sukune and Hozumi-no-Iwayumi. Their mission was to establish further miyake and to administer them, and in the following year miyake were established on Kibi-Kojima. The Nihonshoki explains that miyake were set up in every province of the country but the Kibi miyake were the most important. The fact that the most westerly districts of Kibi, followed by Kojima, were the first to have miyake, indicates that Yamato's policy was to surround central Kibi with miyake which formed centres of government. There are therefore no large tumuli in the western areas of Kibi.

From Yayoi times Kibi-Kojima had been one of the strategic areas of Kibi. The Nihonshoki frequently links the Kibi-no-Omi and later Kibi-no-Anabe-no-Atahe of Kojima (Kibi-no-Shimotsumichi) with the Korean peninsula. The establishment of *miyake* on Kojima in AD 557 indicates how seriously these relations were taken by the authorities in Yamato.

In the *Nihonshoki* there is a confusing reference to Shiraino *miyake* of Kibi which may apply to a person or a small sub-district. Some authorities believe it to be the name of an important personage closely connected with the Kibi *miyake*. Shiraino *miyake* were established in 'the five provinces' of Kibi, thereby implying the inclusion of Mimasaka – northern Kibi, around modern Tsuyama City.

We have seen that one of Kibi's most important associations is with iron, both imported and locally produced. It is unclear when iron was first manufactured in Kibi but many sixth century tumuli of northern Bingo (north-west Kibi) and Mimasaka have been found over the workings of iron mines. It seems fairly certain that iron was produced in the fifth century and that it was one of the main sources of Princess Waka's influence at King Yuryaku's court, creating a power base for their son, Prince Hoshikawa, to mount his coup d'état. Yamato may have established the Shiraino *miyake* to control the supply of iron. The Kojima Miyake supervised maritime affairs while the Shiraino *miyake* are found wherever iron was produced. It is noteworthy that the court sent Soga-no-Iname, a very powerful minister of definite Korean descent and with very strong Korean connections, to expand the *miyake*. This again emphasizes Yamato's acute consciousness of Kibi's strong Korean bias and its need to maintain control.

But was there no one still powerful enough to vie with the Yamato court? The local Omi continued to construct tumuli of the same size as the Omi of Yamato and constant references in the *Nihonshoki* to the Kibi *miyake* without explanation of their significance leads me to believe that they were just deliberately ignored.

The *Nihonshoki* records that in AD 585, during the reign of the Emperor Bidatsu (AD 538–585), the Kibi-no-Amabe-no-Atahe called Hashima was dispatched to Paekche to summon Nichira, a high-born Japanese official, to Yamato to advise the court on its relations with the peninsula. The powerful kingdom of Silla in east Korea had managed to conquer Kaya in AD 562 despite the fact that Paekche and Yamato forces had given support to their Kaya ally. After this defeat five thousand Kayan families emigrated to Japan, many of whom settled in Kibi.

The emperor was naturally anxious to restore Yamato prestige and the power of Kaya both at home and abroad. This was of great importance as he himself was of Puyo/Kayan blood and the majority of his people were also of Puyo/Kayan descent. Nichira, who had long served as a trusted advisor to Paekche on matters of Yamato-Paekche diplomacy, was highly regarded and thought the only person capable of providing direct advice to the Yamato 'Emperor'. The Paekche court was reluctant to let him make the journey but, realising the gravity of the Yamato request, consented to his departure. He travelled with a group of senior Paekche officials and the emperor's personal emissary, the Kibi-no-Amabe-no-Atahe, Hashima. On the journey the party stopped for some time at Kibi Kojima, Hashima's home. (Amabe was Hashima's surname and although his full title included the word Kibi, it seems unlikely that he was descended from the original Omi of Kibi Shimotsumichi [coastal Kibi-Kojima]; the name Amabe is often found in provincial Omi names.) Hashima probably came from a powerful family near the sea and his seniority is obvious from the way in which he was esteemed by the Yamato court and entrusted with Kojima as his fief. During Nichira's sojourn at Kojima the emperor sent the Otomo-no-Muraji, the chief of the imperial palace guard, to honour him. The meeting at Kojima shows how strong Kojima's relations were with Yamato. The guest facilities must have been equivalent to those at the central court which prided itself on its sophistication, for Kojima was clearly one of Yamato's most important bases.

The implication here is that complete Kibi loyalty to the Yamato hegemony was still doubtful and for the other Kibi Omi to lose Kojima support must have been traumatic. Nichira finally conferred with the emperor but advised that Kaya was lost. He was assassinated on his return to Paekche.

The current boundaries of Kojima divide it neatly in two and it is administered by the two modern cities of Kurashiki and the prefectural capital, Okayama. In and before the Edo period, the entire island was under the administration of Bizen province and the Ikeda *daimyo* ('war lords'). At one time a part of Kojima was known as Miyakego, but the ideograms used to write *miyake* differ from those used for the imperial storehouses and lands. The characters are, however, found in the ninth century *Wamyosho*. About thirty years ago, when the serious exca-vation of Heijokyo, the old Asuka capital, began, a wooden tally was discovered. It bore an inscription giving the date of receipt of rice, by way of fealty, from the Miyakego of Kojima. The inscription dated from the Tempyo period (AD 722–784). The use of the modest term *go* indicates that the court of the eighth century was still very aware of Kojima's strategic importance, and the tally recorded details down to village level with a precision unusual for those times. The exact location of the Kojima *miyake* was probably on the eastern end of the island, facing the north. The land in this area has now been reclaimed, but it is possible to see that the bay was long and well sheltered, providing an excellent location for a major port with a fine command of the sea lanes between the island and the mainland.

At Yabataya, on Kojima, a number of large tumuli have been discovered, all with horizontal stone passages leading to the burial chambers. One was so large that, in living memory, a man with an ox could take shelter in it from sudden bad weather. In another, a stone house-shaped coffin was found, inside which were gold heart-shaped earrings. These have since disappeared.

The occupants of these tumuli must have been involved in maritime trade. It is not yet possible to determine whether they are the tumuli of Kibi-no-Amabe-no-Atahe family or of officials sent by the central government to administer the *miyake*. From the size of the tumuli, however, we can be certain that the occupants were of great influence and were probably connected with the Yamato central government. About ten

32. The inland seaway in eastern Kibi. Trading vessels heading for Yamato had to hug the coast here because of strong whirlpools and currents which even today can be perilous to merchant vessels.

kilometres to the east of Miyakego is the mouth of the Asahi River—the narrowest strait between Kojima and the mainland. Here lies a small island called Takashima, where the ruins of a shrine dating from the fifth and sixth centuries were found. This shrine must honour the guardian deity of the Kibi navy, and would have been a station for prayer before its departure on active service. Archaeological research has shown that the shrine ceased to be used at about the time the *miyake* were established in the sixth century. This suggests that it was a shrine of the old clans and was no longer favoured by the new Yamato overlords.

There is an interesting story in the King Nintoku section of the *Nihonshoki* telling of a large poisonous water snake at a fork of the Kawashima River in Kibi. The snake is described as a scourge of the people; travellers passing by were poisoned by it and many died. The district warden, Agata-Mori, another ancestor of the Omi of Kaya, slew the river snake, and at the bottom of the pool he found a cave filled with a 'tribe' of water snakes and these he also killed.

This story, I believe, allegorizes the end of the clan power of Kojima with its powerful Takashima Shrine at the mouth of the Asahi River. The tribes at the bottom of the pool could be a reference to the clan at the head of the bay—the Kibi navy. It is equally plausible that the legend refers to the Puyo/Kayan battle for Kibi, and, interestingly, it is the only reference to Kibi in the King Nintoku section of the *Nihonshoki*. However unreliable the *Nihonshoki* may be, the fact that Kibi-Kojima and later its *miyake* are mentioned so often illustrates the great influence of the area and Yamato sensitivity toward it. The establishment of the Kibi *miyake* probably marked the end of Kibi clan power.

Tatami, Coffins and Cremation

The oldest surviving continuous product from the Tumulus period to the present day in Kibi is tatami floor matting. The mats are about two metres long and one metre wide and today are about seven centimetres thick. The bulk of the tatami mat is made of rough rice straw, tightly compressed, over which is laid a covering of tightly woven *igusa* grass, the edges of which are bound with cloth. The Wamyosho relates that, up to the tenth century, tatami mats were made in sizes varying according to the rank of the owner. The cloth bindings denoted the status of the household. The Queen Regent Jingu-Kogo, mother of King Ojin, is credited with using the *igusa* grass as flooring for the first time on her return from her 'successful conquest' of Korea.

The Korean and Manchurian form of household heating is the *ondol*, which was developed around the third or fourth century BC. The *ondol* system is unique and consists of flues under a stone floor leading from a fixed fireplace on one side of a room to a chimney on the other side. The introduction of *ondol* coincided with the introduction of iron, which enabled wooden residences to be built with greater ease than with the use of bronze and stone tools of earlier periods. The comparatively temperate climate of western Japan is the probable reason why the *ondol* heating system was never used in Japan. Perhaps the ancients found that the thick rice straw padding covered by *igusa* grass matting absorbed and held the warmth of the room, which was created by the use of braziers heated by wood and charcoal. Firepits were also built into the floor filled with ash over which a cauldron bubbled, fuelled by charcoal or wood logs. This is still a popular form of heating. The smoke and fumes escaped through the thatched roofs.

A reference in the *Kojiki* to Queen Jingo Kogo introducing the *igusa* mats is most likely concerned with the art of weaving, which was imported from Kaya at that time. *Igusa* grass grows in Korea and is most abundant in Kibi—even today. The weavers, said to have accompanied Queen Jingo Kogo back from her 'successful conquests', were certainly immigrant exiles or slaves brought by the Puyo/Kayan conquerors in the fourth century AD. Their grass weaving skills would have been well rewarded and admired.

The present Japanese system of covering an entire room with fitted mats dates from the fourteenth century. At the Kanakurayama tumulus at Sawata, in Okayama City, and at the Tsukinowa tumulus, in Kumegun, iron implements were found with vestiges of woven material still upon them. The implements were either bound or wrapped in the material. The thickness of the weave and method of weaving is identical to that found on modern tatami. The material had no joints or nodules as does bamboo, indicating the use of *igusa* grass. The two tumuli with tatami traces date from the fifth century, when Kibi was at its strongest. Products woven from *Igusa* in the tatami style are still manufactured today and it is interesting that the chieftains of the Tumulus period considered them sufficiently important to be included among their funerary trappings for the next world.

On the other hand, pottery coffins (*tokan*), which are no longer produced today, are found in the tombs of the late Tumulus period. These *tokan* were only made in the eastern districts of Kibi, and the greatest number have been found in the north-east around the city we now know as Tsuyama, in Mimasaka. They are buff in colour and fired in the same fashion as Hajiki pottery. They were manufactured in four parts and later assembled into two sections—the lid and the base. The shape of the whole coffin is rectangular or oval. The bases are supported by twenty or more hollow cylindrical legs, like those of a caterpillar; both the legs and the bases are decorated in applied bands of clay-like straps, and at either end of the lid is a lug, with several more along the sides. These lugs were used to attach the lid firmly to the base; viewed from the above and side, the lids look like polyped tortoises with the cross straps of clay suggesting the shell. The average length of a *tokan* is two metres and the width and depth fifty to sixty centimetres; the sides are about four to five centimetres thick, which shows that great skill was required in their firing. *Tokan* are often found in tumuli with horizontal stone chambers. At the Sarayama tumulus in Tsuyama City, a group of seven *tokan* were found in one chamber, while South-east of Mimasaka, in eastern Kibi, is

33. Pottery *tokan* or coffins surrounded by stoneware Sue ceramics *in situ* at time of excavation. The pottery *tokan* were used by the lower classes instead of stone which was costly and expensive to cut. This was a group burial. Vestiges of cinnabar (the elixir of everlasting life) can still be seen on the pottery surface of the coffins. Their shape imitates the stone styles of the grander burials. Laws must have existed to prohibit extravagant tomb burials as the size and contents are small. Reference to such laws is made in the ancient histories of the eighth century.

in another stone chamber a *tokan* and a wooden coffin were found together. It would appear, therefore, that at the end of the Tumulus period, the large tumuli were no longer used as individual graves but had become family mausolea used over generations. Occasionally, among groups of Hajiki type *tokan*, grey coffins made in the higher fired tradition of the Sue potters are found. In the Mimasaka district, however, Sue style coffins are rare and the majority are Hajiki. Southeast of Mimasaka in Kibi is

Oku and the area now known as Bizen. In ancient times the more westerly regions of the neighbouring Hyogo prefecture had close relations with eastern Kibi, particularly with Oku and Bizen, for a number of *tokan* have been found there. In the eastern Bitchu district on the Soja plain, close to Kurashiki City, is the Komorizuka tumulus with its large stone sarcophagus. This dates from the late Tumulus period and has a large horizontal stone passageway leading to the burial chamber. A small Hajiki *tokan* was found near the stone coffin and seems to have been placed there sometime after the main burial. No *tokan* have been found in Bingo – western Kibi – and apart from the western Hyogo finds and a few tortoise-shaped *tokan* at Yamato, Kawachi, Yamashiro and Omi, all other known examples are from Kibi. The tortoise-shaped *tokan* were influenced by the house-shaped stone coffins and

34. A stone sarcophagus in the Komorizuka (bats) tumulus, sixth century AD. Legend has it that this is the tomb of Princess Kuro, granddaughter of Kibitsu Hiko who married the Emperor Nintoku. This cannot be correct, for the dating of the tomb is three hundred or so years later than the suggested dates for Princess Kuro, the 'black princess' of legend.

developed in their own right with characteristics peculiar to their shape, function and period. Where and when they were first produced is still unclear. Stone house-shaped coffins are very numerous in central Kibi, especially in areas where the Shiraino *miyake* were established. The *Nihonshoki* gives the names of the individuals sent from Yamato to administer the Shiraino miyake and lays particular emphasis on Yamato's power and influence in Kibi, but the presence of a number of tortoise-shaped *tokan* in Yamato again resurrects the interminable Japanese debate on where the dominant influence flowed from. There are stylistic differences between Mimasaka and Yamato *tokan*. In the latter, the clay straps are narrower and the manner in which they were attached to the coffin is a little different, and the lugs on the Yamato *tokan* lids are hollow, with holes set into the coffin. Such *tokan* appear to have been made so that long bamboo poles could be placed through the lugs and lids to facilitate carrying. Either the person for whom the *tokan* was made died in Kibi and was taken to Yamato or, more likely, a guild was sent to serve at the Yamato court, some of whose members preferred to be buried in the Kibi tradition.

The practice of transporting coffins over long distances has recently been proven scientifically. The stone coffin in the Komorizuka tumulus in central Kibi has been shown to have come from a quarry in neighbouring Hyogo prefecture, while the bottom half of a coffin found on the top of the Tsukuriyama tumulus came from a quarry on Mt Aso in Kumamoto prefecture hundreds of kilometres away.

The firing technique for such large pottery objects was complicated, requiring great knowledge and skill in kiln heat control. Such expertise would best come from people who knew how to control furnaces, and the iron-makers had the obvious technical ability.

In the later stages of the Tumulus period, very few people were of sufficient status to be buried in hand-hewn stone coffins. Among the ten thousand odd ancient tombs so far discovered in Kibi only about ten such stone coffins have been found. Those who could not afford the luxury of stone were buried in simpler pottery sarcophagi of a similar shape to the stone coffins of people of high rank. *Tokan* made in the Sue style are different from their Hajiki counterparts. They are found in the Yamato, Kibi and Shikoku regions and are not concentrated in any particular area. It is curious that in Yamaguchi and Hiroshima prefectures and in the area known as Bingo, western Kibi, no pottery coffins have been found. This tends to suggest that the style petered out in areas distant from Yamato influence. Sue coffins would have been made in the kilns used to make other Sue vessels. Invariably, Sue coffins are found in areas where the kilns were located, indicating that the occupants of the Sue coffins, like the Hajiki, had some occupational or territorial connection with the kilns.

The Sue house-shaped coffins found in Kibi often have different lids from those found elsewhere, and the gables are much emphasized. The majority of Sue coffins found in Kibi were produced in Oku, near Bizen. The *Engishiki*, a series of volumes describing the customs of the

35. An elaborate Sue ware pedestal jar identical to Korean peninsular prototypes. Made in Kibi by immigrant craftsmen, sixth–seventh century AD. This stoneware vessel would have been filled with food or drink to sustain the deceased in the after-life. Sue stoneware was produced in great quantities in Kibi and exported to Yamato and elsewhere. It is the precursor of Bizen ware for which Okayama/Kibi is famous today.

The National Museum, Tokyo.

provinces, published in AD 927, records that Sue pottery was produced for the court at Oku, in Bizen province, and was of fine quality. It is generally thought that the peak production for Sue ceramics at Oku was during the seventh century and it was during this period that the special coffins were manufactured. Near modern Kurashiki City in Bitchu is the Hoita kiln ruin, where Sue pottery was manufactured in some quantity, and near this kiln, gabled house-shaped coffins have been found. During the seventh century, the Oku and Hoita kilns may have been connected, suggesting that Bitchu and Bizen were under one administration or Shiraino *miyake*. In western Kibi, away from the kilns, no pottery has been found in the later tumuli, which would indicate that the *miyake* of Kibi subdivided regions, and therefore their joint power, by cutting down communication between them.

In areas in Kibi where Hajiki and Sue coffins were produced, the coffin tradition continues even after the end of the Tumulus period. Coffins much smaller in size have been found decorated in both the tortoise, gabled house, and standard style – exact miniatures of the larger prototypes. Some contained cremated remains, showing that traditional coffin styles had been adapted as cinerary boxes. These date from the beginning of the eighth century when burial practices changed radically, from the use of large tombs to cremation, which in turn was superceded by small cinerary interments in groups. Those who cremated their dead were from a social stratum which practised Buddhism. It is evident from the stylistic continuity of votive objects that, when Buddhism reached Kibi, the innovations resulting from the new religion blended into the traditions of past ages in much the same way the earlier Puyo conquerors respected the tumulus traditions of the indigenous people.

During the sixth and seventh centuries, in the domains of the chieftains, there were those who eagerly adapted the new Korean-influenced culture. The people began to engage in free enterprise and through inter-family skirmishes enlarged their land and wealth and thereby gained power. The middle and small-sized tombs of the late Tumulus period are those of this emerging class of meritocratic manufacturers and farmers. They would have regarded the aristocracy with some envy and in death it was their ambition to emulate their superiors; hence their slavish copying and embellishment in clay of the stone coffins of the great. Perhaps the most impressive of these clay coffins was found at Hirafuku in Mimasaka. On this house-shaped coffin one gable-end has a view in relief—in the centre is a figure of a woman in a long skirt with her hair in a top-knot; on either side of her are animals, either foxes or horses feeding from her hands, in the foreground are two spear-like posts and the whole scene is set below three mountain peaks. Local historians like to deduce from this relief that at the time, some of the people were sufficiently independent to engage in individual artistic expression, as found on the coffin end, although the area was ruled by a central Yamato authority controlling the regions of Kibi. This argument I find rather simplistic. I am inclined to think that the decoration has a hidden symbolic meaning, possibly shamanistic or taoist, which currently eludes us.

The Soga in Kibi

As power in Yamato consolidated during the sixth century, the indomitable Korean immigrant family of Soga became increasingly influential. They overshadowed all the immigrant families during the sixth century and the first half of the seventh. The Soga introduced new systems of government and their great strength lay in their absolute control of the country's tax system. It was Soga-no-Iname who, in AD 556, set up the first *miyake* in Kibi – a natural choice, considering Kibi's strong Korean political, cultural and racial bias. The *Nihonshoki* relates that, in AD 574, Soga-no-Umako, son of Iname, was sent by the Emperor Bidatsu (AD 572–585) to Kibi to extend the Shiraino *miyake*. Soga-no-Umako had observed that the original *miyake* system in Kibi, initiated by his father, was not working as well as had been hoped. The *miyake*, as discussed earlier, was a system used to tax the populace and control production but soon after its introduction the people found ways and means of avoiding the levy controls.

Soga-no-Umako employed Itsu-no-Obito, nephew of O-Chin-ni, a descendent of an aristocratic Paekche family settled in Yamato, to tighten Yamato control of the Kibi Shiraino *miyake*. Itsu introduced a new system of census-taking. The old system recorded only the adult males of each family, which created a loophole in tax accountability. The new system, called the *Tahe*, recorded all members of all families and the extent of their possessions. This forerunner of the *Ritsu-ryo* civil codes introduced in AD 701 specified accepted social behaviour, tax and punishment. From the *Nihonshoki* account, it is fairly clear that the new census was designed by Soga-no-Umako while visiting Kibi in AD 574. Itsu administered the new system and reported directly to the central government, and was personally answerable to Soga-Umako, the head of all the Korean immigrant families, and prime minister. He was so successful that he was given the name Shirai-no-obito-Itsu and granted the title *Tatsukasa*—'overlord of all the *miyake*'. Here again is an example of a person of noble Korean ancestry from Yamato assuming a position of great importance in Kibi.

The Arrival of Buddhism

Buddhism was formally introduced to Paekche from south China in AD 384, twelve years after its arrival in the northern kingdom of Koguryo and fifteen years after the Puyo/Kayan conquest of Japan Wa. Paekche wasted little time in adopting Chinese culture. During the reign of King Kunch'ogo a history was written, known as the *Sogi*; this was quickly followed by several others; most notable among these was the Paekche *Pon'gi*, in which frequent contacts with the branch states of Wa are described.

In one chapter is an account of the great Paekche scholar Wang-in (Wani in Japanese) and his introduction of the *Confucian Analects* to Wa in AD 405. The Koreans also attribute to him the transmission to Wa of the *Sen-ji-mon* ('Confucian Book of One Thousand Characters'), but this claim is contradicted by the Japanese in the *Kojiki*, which gives credit for this to the other great contemporary scholar, Ajiki, who is also said to have presented horses and weavers to the Wa emperor. Ajiki was the Achi-no-Omi of the *Nihonshoki*; although some scholars think that Ajiki and Achi-no-Omi are separate persons, I disagree, for the accounts of their achievements and the proximity of their dates are too similar. The introduction of the *Confucian Analects* coinciding with the Puyo/Kayan conquests is very well timed; the substance of Confucianism is respect for elders in the family, superiors in public life and for the divine right of kings. Through this philosophy, people were taught the value of tradition, institutions and ceremonies.

Confucian thought placed profound trust in the power of example as the basis of sound government. If we examine Kibi in the fourth and fifth centuries, we can see clearly how the Puyo/Kayan conquerors put the new philosophy into practice. A new culture was built upon the foundations of the old; nowhere is this more clearly demonstrated than in the construction of the tumuli. The old traditions were kept and moulded to suit the concepts of the newcomers, who grew to coexist over a period of time and intermarry with the indigenous race.

The Korean and Japanese histories are almost in agreement in their description of the King of Paekche's presentation of a gilt bronze image of Shakyamuni—Gautama, the Lord Buddha—to the Emperor Kimmei in AD 552. This gift was carried to Yamato by ambassadors of the highest rank and was accompanied by flags, umbrellas and donations of volumes of sutras and incense. The King of Paekche also presented a tablet and, through the ambassadors, offered a dissertation on the merits of the Buddhist doctrine. The *Nihonshoki* records that the Emperor 'leapt with joy', but was unable to decide whether or not he should accept the new religion. Subsequent discussions with his ministers plunged Yamato into internal rivalry with political and religious repercussions. The new faith posed a real threat to the chieftains of the old Yamato clans, whose status and prestige was founded on their descent from ancestral spirits. The Buddhist faith claimed to have greater powers than those of the ancestral spirits upon which the chieftains based their authority.

The Soga family, who descended, as did the Emperor, from the Puyo/Kayan conquerors of AD 369, approved the new religion. Nevertheless, the *Nihonshoki* reports that the emperor was careful to heed the advice of the old Yamato hereditary chieftains and feared incurring the wrath of their tutelary gods. He therefore had the Paekche gifts given to Soga-no-Iname, who agreed to worship the Buddha as an experiment. Iname took the statue to his home and erected a Buddhist shrine called *Kogen-ji* which is regarded by some as the first in Japan. In the next year a plague afflicted Yamato, and the tribal chieftains wasted little time in trying to persuade the emperor that the pestilence should be attributed to the vengeance of the ancestral spirits in their disgust at the introduction of an alien religion. As a result, the precious statue was thrown into the Naniwa Canal. Shortly afterwards two great priests from Paekche were sent to Yamato to help solve this problem and forty years later Buddhism finally received imperial sanction.

This version of events from the *Nihonshoki* is

disingenuous, and although it may be based on historical memories, I am confident that it is the result of deliberate fabrication. We should not overlook the fact that it was during the reign of Emperor Kimmei that the Korean kingdom of Silla finally overran Kaya and severed Japan's close link with its Korean neighbour and cultural benefactor. Soga-no-Iname's daughter was the wife of the Emperor Kimmei and their son became the thirty second Emperor, Sushin (AD 523–592). If the Emperor Sushin was really born in AD 523, it is easy to visualize the immense power of the Soga clan, whose leader was the imperial father-in-law during the first half of the sixth century. By the time of Iname's death, the Soga clan had become the greatest force in the land and had firmly grasped the reins of government. Upon Sushin's death in AD 592, his sister Suiko became the first Yamato empress in her own right. She was previously married to her half-brother, the Emperor Bidatsu. Her support of the Soga is recorded in the Nihonshoki: 'I am of the Soga clan; therefore, I do not, if at all possible, object to anything said by the Omi (Soga-no-Imako)'. It is accepted that, by AD 587, the Soga had vanquished the old chieftains of Yamato who had advocated the rejection of Buddhism and had employed numerous imported Paekche artisans to construct the first integrated temple complex in Japan, Hoko-Ji, from whence Buddhism spread unimpeded.

Surely it is no coincidence that, three years after the King of Paekche's presentation of the gilt bronze Buddha to the Emperor Kimmei, his own father-in-law, Soga-no-Iname, who had treasured the image only to have it confiscated and thrown into the Naniwa Canal, was sent to Kibi to establish the Shiraino *miyake*. It would appear from the chronicles that Soga-no-Iname dwelt in Kibi for a period and at this time he may have encouraged the dissemination of the new religion while safely beyond the interference of the old Yamato chieftains and among the powerful Korean-biased chieftains of Kibi. Iname's journey and sojourn in Kibi would have coincided with the beginning of the immigration of the five thousand displaced Korean families; their links with the old Hata and Kaya clans of Kibi were very strong.

I cannot accept that the Paekche king would have presumed to have made the presentation of the image of Buddha and sutras in AD 552 had the religion not already been practiced among many of the upper class for many years. The Soga's direct connections with Paekche have never been in question. Soga-no-Iname had become the Japanese Emperor Kimmei's father-in-law and this would indicate that the King of Paekche had waited until the most opportune moment to make his presentation. He knew full well the strength of the old Yamato chieftains and the still delicate position of the new Puyo/Kayan imperial system, which by this time had been present in Yamato for a little over one hundred years, during which the court and the imperial succession had been plagued with dissention. In fact, the Emperor Kimmei's reign was the first stable period since his father Keitai had wrested power from the succession of the 'Five Kings of Wa' which ended with the King Buretsu's death in AD 506.

My view that Buddhism arrived in Japan much

earlier than AD 552 is supported by the ancient record of the appearance in AD 522 of Sumatah (Shiba Tatto in Japanese) in Yamato; though he ultimately failed in his attempt to preach Buddhism among the common people, who rejected the foreign theology, his three daughters later became the first Buddhist nuns. It is particularly significant that the Emperor Sushin, whose mother was Soga-Iname's daughter, was born in AD 523. The Soga family were thus Buddhist activists from an early age, and dedicated to the Lord Buddha's prophecy that the doctrines should spread in an easterly direction; they used their imperial connections wherever possible.

During the fifth century, while Yamato was in the process of becoming the most easterly point of the Puyo/Kayan sphere of influence, Kibi maintained constant contact with the Korean peninsula, and discoveries from the many tumuli of the period endorse this. It is possible that the new Buddhist faith arrived in Kibi at this time and was adopted by some of the new aristocracy, until it finally gained the attention of the Soga clan in Yamato. They embraced the new religion as a mark of distinction and proof of a mainland sophistication over their rivals, the old clan chieftains of Yamato. How, precisely, Buddhism was transmitted to and practiced in Kibi is impossible to determine, but surely it would have found its base among the leaders of the new Hata and Kaya clans of central Kibi and the prosperous iron casters of Niiyama and Hata villages. The spread of Buddhism brought a new dimension to Kibi religious thinking. The old neo-shaman Shintoism did not die, but coexisted with the new faith. As Buddhism slowly took hold, it absorbed many old popular beliefs and was looked to for protection from ill health and for an amelioration of the rigours of life. That it offered protection of both the king and the common people virtually guaranteed its ultimate acceptance.

From the late fifth century, the tumuli in Kibi became smaller, with the addition of new styles of burial chamber and the gradual emergence of pottery coffins. The power of the chieftains was trimmed and the rapid rise in importance of a new farmer-merchant class is seen in the greater number of smaller tombs found in the valleys, on islands, the sides of hills and in centres of population where the newcomers had settled.

The earliest temple in Kibi was probably Hatabara at Hata village, now a part of Soja City. Only ruins have survived and from the tiles discovered in the surrounding fields we can date the temple to 630 AD. The temple had a tall pagoda, judging from its enormous foundation stone; the stone was cleft to support a square main pillar and twenty other pillar base stones have been found, as well as the remains of a circular wooden pillar. The oldest roof end-tiles made at the site appear to date from the late sixth or early seventh century. The outside rim of the circular tile end is undecorated, but the inner section is decorated with an eight petal simple lotus with flat petals; the stamen section of the lotus is small and has five anther nodules; between each petal is a small dot, an unusual feature and as yet, no other examples have been found. Similar Kibi tiles have been found close to the Terayama tumulus in Tsukubo-gun in northern Kibi and another was excavated from the Sue kilns at Oku

Photo: Courtesy of author

36. A Korean gold figure of the Taoist philosopher Noja (Chinese: Lao Tzu). Height: 3.3 cm. Discovered at the ruins of the enormous Hatabara Temple complex in central Kibi; constructed c. 630 AD. This figure has been studied by Tsukuba University in Tokyo and the gold found to be of Korean origin. Its presence in Kibi may prove that Taoism was brought to Japan by Korean settlers and practiced in Kibi. The very term Shinto, or 'The Way of the Gods' was introduced a few years after Buddhism and suggests inspiration from Taoist sources. The Hatabara Temple was one of the first Buddhist temples built in Kibi and Japan. It is possible that Buddhism was first tested in Kibi by the powerful Soga family, immigrants from Korea, who were the ministers of finance and closely related to the Yamato royal family and very influential in Kibi among their fellow immigrant Kayan and Paekche Koreans. The faith later spread to Yamato.

Private collection.

Photo: The Birmingham Museum of Art

37. A Korean early sixth century AD (Three Kingdoms period) gilt bronze figure of Buddha. Height 7 cm. Discovered in Kibi. Small images such as this were intended as personal objects of devotion. Worshipped in Shrines at home or easily transported, these dimunitive works were a key component in the dissimination of sacred iconography both within Korea and Japan. This figure was probably carried to Kibi by Korean immigrants who assisted in the extension of technological advances, beliefs and cultural forms within greater Japan.

The Birmingham Museum of Art, Alabama, USA.

in eastern Kibi. Similarly simple finial designs have been found at Shitenno-ji Temple in Osaka and at Koryuji Temple in Kyoto. These temples, however, are thought to have been built in the late Asuka period. All these designs reflect the style of early Paekche temple tiles, particularly those found at some of the ruins at Puyo. Excavations of the Sue kilns at Oku unearthed a great many tiles, including some large gargoyle designs. They are decorated in the same simple eight petal lotus style, but the ends of the petals were square, the separating dots are differently placed and the stamen and anther pattern is similarly small and simple, with five dots. The outside rim differs and contains a design of circles separated by cross-hatching. At first glance the large tiles are much more definite in style and conform to Asuka patterns. They are all, however, heavily influenced by Paekche, and are arguably the work of the artisans who travelled from Paekche, and later Koguryo, to Japan, and settled in the areas where the new temples were being constructed.

At Misaki, in Maniwa-gun, Mimasaka, northern Kibi, are some ruins of the Hakuho period (AD 645–710) which are known as the Gotan Temple ruins. There is a stone pillar at this site with a carved inscription stating that this was a Shiraino *miyake*. There is no further evidence to support the validity of the inscription, but its presence at the site of a very early temple conjures up a number of interesting possibilities. The Soga clan's dual connection with the establishment of the first Shiraino *miyake* in Kibi and the introduction of Buddhism leads me to suggest that the existence of this pillar supports my earlier contention that Buddhism entered Kibi at a much earlier date than hitherto imagined and that the first Buddhist shrines were probably erected at the sites of the various headquarters of the Shiraino *miyake* directly under Soga control. Overlords such as Itsu-no-Obito would have been practicing Buddhists in the Soga tradition; those who embraced the Soga's faith would have been given positions of great importance and would have prospered. It is also likely that the first great temple complexes were constructed upon the sites of the early shrines at the Shiraino *miyake*. Archaeologists will surely confirm this in the future and, through analysis of the temple ruins, locate the Shiraino *miyake* and their areas of influence.

At the Terado Temple ruins at Miyoshi in Bingo, western Kibi, some other unusual Kibi-style roof tiles have been discovered. At the base of the tile ends is a triangular projection depicting a rain-drop. This style has also been found at the Osaki Temple ruins in western Okayama City and as far away as Jin-mon-ji Temple in Kumo City, Shimane prefecture, on the Japan Sea coast. Kibi seems to have influenced other areas in Buddhism as in many other aspects. When the first Buddhist temples were being constructed in Kibi, most Kibi people were still being buried in the traditional fashion, for there is no evidence of Buddhist influence in funeral practices. Gradually, however, the tombs became smaller and it seems obvious that the greater part of labour resources was being re-directed into the construction of temples. According to ancient records, between the mid sixth century and the end of the Nara period in AD 793 over seventy large

38. A fine Korean Paekche-inspired roof tile from early
temple ruins in eastern Kibi. Magnificent tile and roof gable
ends have been found all over Kibi. The early temple ruins all
display close design similarities with those of Paekche in
Korea. This shows that the earliest Buddhist practices in Japan
were influenced greatly by Paekche, which of course had,
itself, been influenced by China. The strong Paekche styles
were later softened into prevailing Japanese taste.

The Kurashiki City Office.

39.   A Korean Paekche-influenced roof tile probably made at the Hoita kilns in central Kibi; seventh century AD. The Hoita kilns were totally destroyed when the Shinkansen railway line was constructed in the early 1970s. Much material was excavated beforehand and evidence came to light of vast temple construction in Kibi. The products from the Hoita kilns have been found as far away as Yamato and the Japan Sea areas.

The Kurashiki City Office.

temples were constructed in the Kibi region. Many of them are grouped closely together, some being only a few hundred metres apart. In Okayama City, the ruins of the Shoda and Akada temples are only a kilometre apart on a north-south line. Four kilometres east of these are the Shishi-Ama Temple ruins and this pattern also occurs in Bingo and elsewhere where new centres of commerce had been established.

Obviously, the descendants of the original Kibi chieftains did not enjoy the immense power of their ancestors, but they were still influential. There must have been some advantage to be gained from the construction of temples. The Soga probably granted a tax exemption of which the chieftains took advantage. Through the construction of temples with an effective government subsidy, the Kibi chieftains were able, as in the past with the huge tumuli, to demonstrate their power and sophistication. That the temples were built on a colossal scale shows that the chieftains had not lost their pride, for they built as many as they could, donating their own land and property, thereby probably reducing the burden of direct taxes. The temples, temple land and the priesthood were all administered by the chieftains, but the new laws of the mid-eighth century made land tenure onerous and restricted new land ownership to three succeeding generations, after which it reverted to the state. Suddenly the construction of temples ceased, and once again Kibi was dominated by Yamato which might seem sad and poignant when one considers that for so long it had been Yamato's equal, mentor and, more than once, its master.

The reader has journeyed with me through many hundreds of years up and down the Inland Sea, in and out of the ancient histories and much has been achieved. Much, however, remains to be learnt, particularly of the relationship between Kibi and Yamato in both their historical and artistic roles. As with Korean history, the fourth and fifth centuries AD in Japan are the periods least understood, but we can be proud of one very important point—that, as hard as those writers and fabricators of early history tried to obliterate all memory of the Puyo and the power of Kibi, they ultimately failed.

What will be found under the soil to further dignify Kibi's historical legacy remains to be seen, but until the Japanese Imperial Household—and other government agencies—are persuaded to open all the so-called 'Imperial Mausolea' for proper archaeological research, any conclusions can only be shrouded in mist.

The boast of heraldry, The pomp of power,
And all that beauty, All that wealth e'er gave,
Await like th' inevitable hour.
The paths of glory lead but to the grave.

Elegy Written in a Country Churchyard, viii-ix
Thomas Gray (1716–1771)

Ancient Chronology

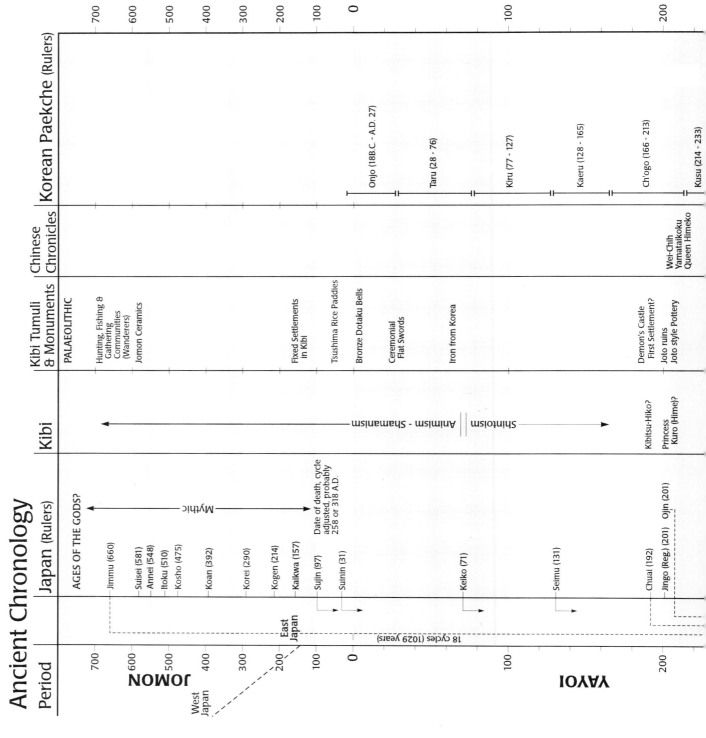

Period	Japan (Rulers)	Kibi	Kibi Tumuli & Monuments	Chinese Chronicles	Korean Paekche (Rulers)

AGES OF THE GODS?

JOMON — 700, 600, 500, 400, 300, 200, 100, 0

West Japan / East Japan

YAYOI — 100, 200

18 cycles (1029 years)

Mythic

Jimmu (660)
Suisei (581)
Annei (548)
Itoku (510)
Kosho (475)
Koan (392)
Korei (290)
Kogen (214)
Kaikwa (157)
Sujin (97)
Suinin (31)

Date of death, cycle adjusted, probably 258 or 318 A.D.

Keiko (71)
Seimu (131)
Chuai (192)
Jingo (Reg.) (201) Ojin (201)

Animism - Shamanism ‖ Shintoism

Kibitsu-Hiko?
Princess Kuro (Hime)?

PALAEOLITHIC

Hunting, Fishing & Gathering Communities (Wanderers)
Jomon Ceramics
Fixed Settlements in Kibi
Tsushima Rice Paddies
Bronze Dotaku Bells
Ceremonial Flat Swords
Iron from Korea
Demon's Castle First Settlement?
Joto ruins Joto style Pottery

Wei-Chih Yamataikoku Queen Himeko

700, 600, 500, 400, 300, 200, 100, 0, 100, 200

Onjo (18B.C. - A.D. 27)
Taru (28 - 76)
Kiru (77 - 127)
Kaeru (128 - 165)
Ch'ogo (166 - 213)
Kusu (214 - 233)

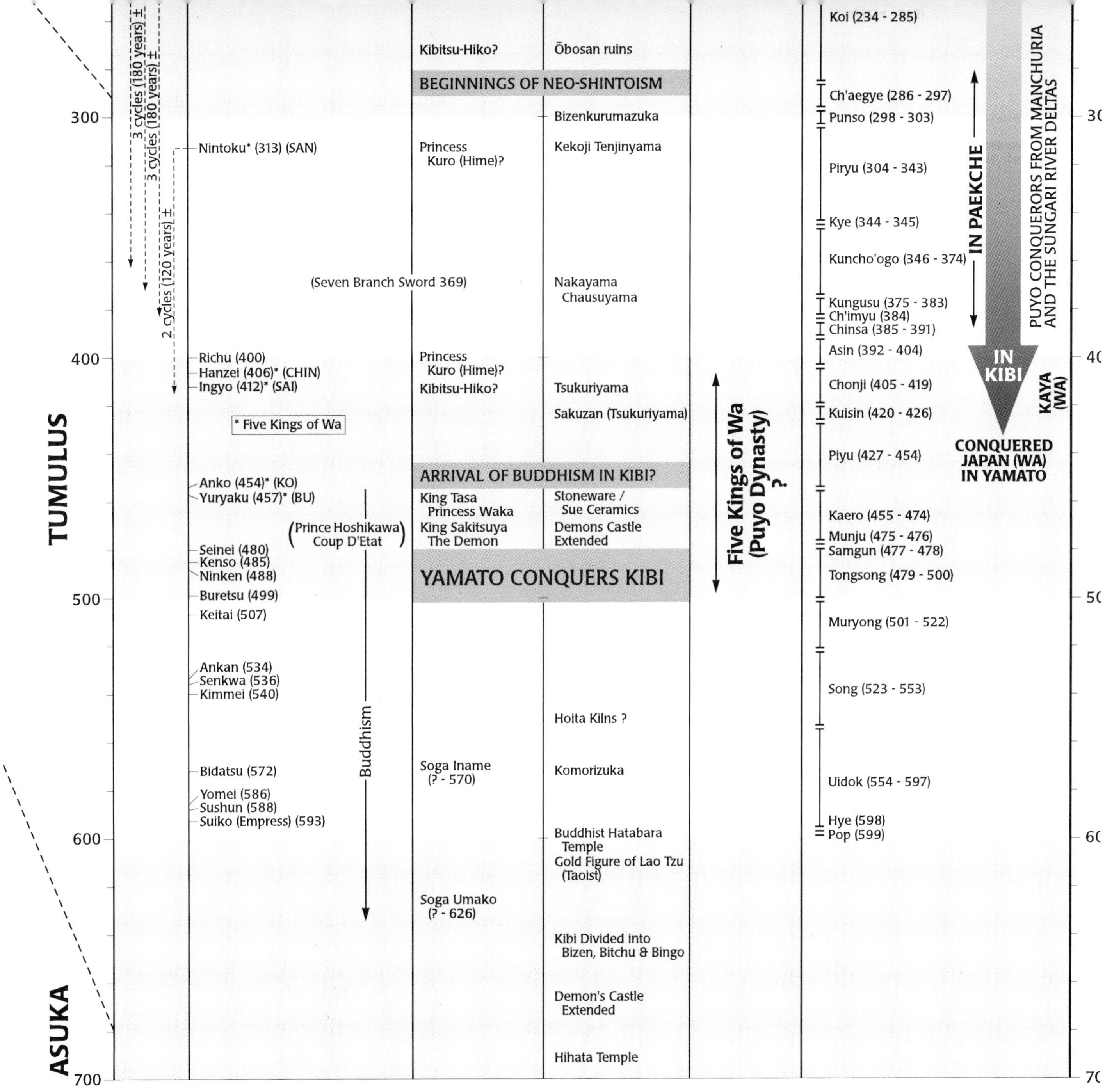

Koi (234 - 285)

PUYO CONQUERORS FROM MANCHURIA AND THE SUNGARI RIVER DELTAS

IN PAEKCHE

IN KIBI

KAYA (WA)

CONQUERED JAPAN (WA) IN YAMATO

Ch'aegye (286 - 297)
Punso (298 - 303)
Piryu (304 - 343)
Kye (344 - 345)
Kuncho'ogo (346 - 374)
Kungusu (375 - 383)
Ch'imyu (384)
Chinsa (385 - 391)
Asin (392 - 404)
Chonji (405 - 419)
Kuisin (420 - 426)
Piyu (427 - 454)
Kaero (455 - 474)
Munju (475 - 476)
Samgun (477 - 478)
Tongsong (479 - 500)
Muryong (501 - 522)
Song (523 - 553)
Uidok (554 - 597)
Hye (598)
Pop (599)

Five Kings of Wa (Puyo Dynasty) ?

Ōbosan ruins	Kibitsu-Hiko?		(Seven Branch Sword 369)	Nintoku* (313) (SAN)
BEGINNINGS OF NEO-SHINTOISM	**BEGINNINGS OF NEO-SHINTOISM**			
Bizenkurumazuka	Princess Kuro (Hime)?			Richu (400)
Kekoji Tenjinyama				Hanzei (406)* (CHIN)
				Ingyo (412)* (SAI)
Nakayama Chausuyama				* Five Kings of Wa
Tsukuriyama	Princess Kuro (Hime)?			
Sakuzan (Tsukuriyama)	Kibitsu-Hiko?			Anko (454)* (KO)
				Yuryaku (457)* (BU)
ARRIVAL OF BUDDHISM IN KIBI?	King Tasa		(Prince Hoshikawa) Coup D'Etat	
Stoneware / Sue Ceramics	Princess Waka			Seinei (480)
Demons Castle Extended	King Sakitsuya			Kenso (485)
	The Demon			Ninken (488)
YAMATO CONQUERS KIBI				Buretsu (499)
				Keitai (507)
				Ankan (534)
				Senkwa (536)
				Kimmei (540)
Hoita Kilns ?	Soga Iname (? - 570)	Buddhism →		Bidatsu (572)
Komorizuka				Yomei (586)
Buddhist Hatabara Temple	Soga Umako (? - 626)			Sushun (588)
Gold Figure of Lao Tzu (Taoist)				Suiko (Empress) (593)
Kibi Divided into Bizen, Bitchu & Bingo				
Demon's Castle Extended				
Hihata Temple				

3 cycles (180 years) ±
3 cycles (180 years) ±
2 cycles (120 years) ±

TUMULUS

ASUKA

300
400
500
600
700

111

40. What other secrets do the misty hills of Kibi hold?

GLOSSARY

Achi-no-Omi. A Korean prince who is thought by early Japanese historians to be the descendant of the Chinese Han emperors (206 BC–AD 220). Achi-no-Omi probably accompanied the Puyo conquerors to Japan in AD 369. He is thought to have presented the emperor with the seven branch sword now enshrined at Isonokami Shrine in Yamato. He was the ancestor of the iron making and weaving guilds of Kaya and Hata peoples and is the guardian deity of modern Kurashiki City.

Aki (Gun). A part of western Kibi now in eastern Hiroshima prefecture.

Ankan. Twenty-seventh emperor of Japan. Reigned AD 531–535. Sent forces to Korea to support Paekche in its war against Silla.

Arai Hakuseki. Celebrated Edo historian (1657–1721) who formed many interesting theories on the whereabouts of the Yamatai and Toma kingdoms. His enlightened views on the two earliest histories of Japan were extremely advanced for the age in which he lived. He became a counsellor to the Tokugawa Shogun, Tsunayoshi.

Asahi River. One of three great rivers of Kibi, which flows through Okayama City.

ashi. A marsh reed. Ancient Yayoi rice growing settlers positioned their paddy fields wherever the reed grew in abundance.

Ashimori. A town in Bitchu, central Kibi. Mentioned frequently in the *Nihonshoki* and *Kojiki* in connection with the reigns of Emperors Nintoku and Ojin. A palace is said to have been built at Ashimori. The Demon's Castle ruins are to be found on the summit of hills to the side of the town.

Asuka. The residence of King Ritchu (AD 400–405). The Asuka period (AD 552–645) was greatly influenced by Korea. Asuka was the headquarters of the powerful Korean Soga clan. Asuka town is situated at the southern point of the Yamato Plain.

Atahe (or **Aya**). Korean immigrants who settled in Yamato and were controlled by Achi-no-Omi. The Aya were closely connected with the Hata and Kaya people, all from the Han tribes of southern Korea.

Awaji Island situated on the Inland Sea between Kobe and Tokushima. In ancient mythology Awaji was the first island created by the gods Izanagi and Izanami. The island almost encloses the eastern end of the Inland Sea.

azo be. A guild of iron workers which came from Korea and settled in the hills overlooking central Kibi and modern Ashimori town. The Azo were iron casters and manufactured domestic and agricultural equipment, nails and temple bells. The Azo were not involved in the manufacture of weaponry. The modern village of Azo flanks the Chisui River near Ashimori town. The predominant patronym of the Azo is Hayashi, derived from the Korean Lin.

Be. The term **be** is derived from the Pu (bu) of Puyo, who were the horse-riding conquerors of Japan in AD 369. In ancient times the term meant an hereditary guild. There were **amabe** ('fishermen'), **oribe** ('weavers'), **tabe** ('farmers'). Local Omi presented fealty to the central court in loans of specialized *be* member craftsmen.

Bingo. The western part of ancient Kibi, now a part of Hiroshima prefecture. The largest city in Bingo is Fukuyama.

Bidatsu. Thirtieth Emperor of Japan. Reigned AD 572–585. During his reign the powerful Soga family, which had earlier imported Buddhism, fell out with the old clan chieftains of Yamato over the acceptance of the new religion. Buddhist votive deities were thrown into the Haniwa Canal. The emperor, on advice from the Soga, sent several military expeditions to Korea to aid the small kingdom of Kaya, which had been invaded by Silla. These were not successful, and were the last such attempts by Japan to exert its will on the Korean peninsula for some hundreds of years.

Bitchu. The central part of ancient Kibi, now a part of Okayama prefecture. The plain between the Takahashi and Asahi rivers is believed to have been the hub of ancient Kibi power. Today Bitchu is dominated by Kurashiki City.

Bizen. The eastern part of ancient Kibi, now a part of Okayama prefecture. Formally, it was part of Kibi Kamitsumichi. Now at Imbe there is a well-known pottery centre with traditions going back to the Sue kilns at Samukaze. The largest city in Bizen is Okayama.

Black Princess. See **Kurohime**.

Chugoku. The district comprising the five prefectures of Tottori, Shimane, Okayama, Hiroshima and Yamaguchi.

cinnabar. Red mercuric sulfide, vermilion. Used in the Yayoi period to decorate pottery. Thought by the ancients to be the elixir of everlasting life.

Dewa. Part or district of Niigata prefecture in northern Japan.

dotaku. Bronze bells reproduced from mainland prototypes probably introduced from Korea. *Dotaku* were symbols of power and are associated with the Yamato district which seems to have distributed them as a means of dispensing favours. *Dotaku* were cast and are often decorated with symbols similar to hieroglyphics. They were probably used in religious rites during the mid-Yayoi period. Some authorities believe they may have been used as time pieces. *Dotaku* were buried on lookout sites over the sea or rich fertile deltas. Some crude pottery *dotaku* have been found in Kibi.

Echigo. Part or district of Niigata prefecture in northern Japan.

Ehime. A prefecture in north-west Shikoku Island.

ento haniwa. Chimney-shaped *haniwa* used as decorative devices in Yayoi cemeteries. Often decorated with incised bands. Offering jars were sometimes placed upon them.

Five kings of Wa. A 'succession' of five kings as described in

Five kings of Wa. A 'succession' of five kings as described in the Chinese history Sung-shu. The Chinese names for the kings are: San, Chin, Sai, Ko and Bu. These are thought to correspond with the Nihonshoki-named emperors: Nintoku, Hanzai, Ingyo, Ankyo and Yuryaku. The dates with relevant cycle adjustments correspond to AD 421–502. The Chinese describe the kings as tribute-payers and receivers of Chinese titles, which they greatly valued.

Fukuyama. City in eastern Hiroshima prefecture and largest in Bingo, western Kibi.

fundo. Small clay tablets with fanciful facial decorations similar in many ways to decorations found on the bronze *dotaku* bells. The *fundo* are believed to have been endowed with magic powers in averting evil and bringing good luck to their holder. *Fundo* are unique to Kibi, although a very few have been found in other areas such as Shimane and the coast of Osaka Bay; they are all thought to have been manufactured in Kibi.

Gemmyo. Empress, forty-third ruler of Japan. Reigned AD 708–714. Responsible for the compilation of Japan's first histories, the *Kojiki* (AD 712) and the *Fudoki* (AD 713).

Genkai. Sea situated north-northwest of Kyushu, also known as the Genkai *nada* or Kyushu *nada*.

Gishi Wa Jin Den. See Wei-Chih.

Go. Chinese Wu. A Chinese dynasty which was overthrown in AD 280. The term Go, however, continued in popular use until AD 589. Achi-no-Omi and his son are alleged to have been sent to Go by the Emperor Ojin.

Gun. Common term for district. First introduced as part of the Taika reforms (AD 645–649) when the country was divided into sixty-six provinces.

Haiji. Term used to describe a ruin or place of former occupation i.e., Hata Bara (temple name) Haiji.

hajiki. Brittle buff-coloured pottery used for domestic purposes during the Yayoi and Tumulus periods. It differs from the later Sue ware in that it was fired in open fires rather than kilns. *Haniwa* are a derivative of *hajiki*. This pottery was produced by the Haji-be (guild).

Hakuho. Era name. The *Nihonshoki* uses the term Hakuji, which corresponds to AD 645–710, in place of Hakuho. Hakuho means white phoenix and Hakuji, white pheasant.

Han. Chinese dynasty corresponding to 206 BC–AD 220. The name can also be read in Japanese as Aya. Also the name of tribes in south Korea.

haniwa. Pottery cylinders on top of which were placed clay representations of animals, human figures and objects of everyday use such as pots, quivers, houses etc. The *haniwa* were placed around the outside of tumuli and according to early

histories, were a substitute for live human immolation.

Hanzei. Eighteenth king of Japan, son of Nintoku. There is some doubt as to whether he lived at all. In all probability, he was a 'padding' monarch for the convenience of the compilers of the early histories.

hatabe. A guild (*be*) of immigrant weavers and iron makers from the Han tribes of south Korea which settled in Kibi probably after the Puyo occupation of AD 369. Achi-no-Omi was the patron of this guild.

Heijokyo. The Chinese-style grid pattern city, west of Nara. Residence of the imperial family, AD 709–784.

Hieda-no-Are. Dictated the history of Japan from memory to Ono Yasumaro, who wrote it down. Her prodigious memory enabled many of the ancient traditions to be recorded in the *Kojiki* (AD 712).

Himiko. Queen of Yamatai, the largest of the Kingdoms of Wa (reigned AD 180–248). Described in detail by the Chinese historians of the Wei dynasty in the Wei Chih, but not recorded in the early Japanese histories. Himiko was a great shaman priestess and held magical powers. According to the Chinese, she was buried in an enormous tumulus and was succeeded by another priestess named Iryo. Her tumulus has yet to be discovered.

Hiuchi Nada. A large coastal basin in north Shikoku, opposite Bingo, eastern Kibi.

Hoita. A small place north-east of Kurashiki City where there were ruins of an ancient tile manufacturing Sue pottery kiln. These ruins were destroyed during the construction of the Shinkansen railway.

Hoshikawa. Son of twenty-first King Yuryaku and Kibi Princess Waka. The *Nihonshoki* describes his attempted coup d'état after his father's death in AD 479. His half-brother Seimei ascended the throne as twenty-second emperor in AD 480.

Ikeda. The *daimyo* war-lord family of Bizen, eastern Kibi, which controlled Bizen from 1632 until the Meiji restoration in 1868.

Inukai-no-Takeru. Retainer and servant of Prince Kibitsu Hiko, whose dog was fed the head of the demon of Kibi.

Isaseri-Hiko-no-Mikoto. Former name of Prince Kibitsu Hiko. The Nihonshoki describes him as the son of King Korei (290 – 215 BC), the seventh king. He was most likely the embodiment of many characters, and in terms of his Kibi accomplishments, he has been made the single personification of many local heroes and deeds. He was probably Korean and one of the first conquering governors or rulers. His tomb could well be one of the two colossal tumuli in central Kibi. The *Kojiki* credits him with the conquest of Izumo. It could be that the title Kibitsu Hiko was hereditary, which might explain same of the confusion surrounding him.

Isonokami. A well-known Yamato Shinto shrine, said to have been built by the tenth king, Sujin, in 72 BC. The seven branch Paekche manufactured sword with an inscription and date corresponding to AD 369 is kept at this shrine.

Izumi. One of the provinces of Yamato.

Izumo. One of the Wa kingdoms situated in modern Shimane prefecture. It was the most difficult kingdom to be conquered by the invading forces from Yamato in the post-Puyo period. Izumo's position within the Yayoi period is the subject of reappraisal due to a recent discovery of bronze swords. A cache of over three hundred swords was discovered in 1985, equal to the total number of Yayoi bronze swords found to date throughout Japan. More recently, a cache of *dotaku* bronze bells has also been discovered nearby.

Jimmu. The first king of Japan (660–585 BC). He is reputed to have conquered Japan in an easterly direction from the domains of his etherial ancestors in present day Miyazaki prefecture. The *Nihonshoki* and the *Kojiki* both describe his exploits in great detail. He is said to have penetrated Kibi where he dwelt for several years preparing for his attack on Yamato, which, after several defeats, was successful. His Yamato palace was erected at Kashiwabara, at the foot of Mt Unebi. The eastern conquests of Jimmu are a very neat allegory of the conquests and occupation of the Puyo people from Korea in AD 369. The compilers of the early histories distorted the truth and dates by seventeen cycles of sixty years. Miyazaki could well have been the site of the first major skirmish between the Puyo and a Japanese Wa kingdom. The route of the Jimmu conquests, as described in the *Nihonshoki*, is probably fairly close to the path the Puyo conquerors took. The position of Kibi in the overall campaign is made very clear.

Jingu Kogo. Queen Regent, wife of fourteenth king, Chuai (AD 149–220). Both the early histories credit her with the conquest of Korea in AD 200. Her son Ojin was born in Tsukushi (northern Kyushu) on her return from Korea. This conquest and birth are an obvious inversion of the truth and again are allusions to the Puyo conquests of the fourth century. A three-cycle adjustment forward neatly places Ojin's birth ten years after the Puyo conquest of AD 369.

Jinshin-no-Ran. The civil war of AD 672.

Jomon. The prehistoric period, which lasted about 12,000 years until the third or fourth century BC. The name is derived from the cord (Jo) pattern (mon) found on the early earthenware pottery. The Jomon people are believed to have been a mixture of proto-European and later South Sea immigrant people. They were the ancestors of the Ainu who today dwell in Hokkaido and are of Caucasian stock.

Jotoshiki. A Yayoi style of pottery named after the site in Kurashiki City, where the first examples were discovered. Jotoshiki is a term which generally refers to jars on long, tall, pedestal feet.

Kagawa. Prefecture in north-east Shikoku, facing the Inland Sea and Kibi.

kanji. Chinese ideograms adapted to Japanese phonetics.

Kawachi. One of the five provinces of Yamato.

Kaya. One of the ancient kingdoms of southern Korea which was conquered by Silla in AD 562. In the early Tumulus period it was probably the headquarters of Wa, from where the branch states on the Japanese archipelago were controlled. Kaya was first conquered and occupied by the Puyo, prior to their invasion of the archipelago in AD 369. Many Kayan immigrants settled in Kibi after the Puyo and Silla conquests. Kaya was the home of many of the Han peoples including the Aya and the Hata. Achi-no-Omi was probably a Kayan prince.

keisho haniwa. Figurines of clay placed on clay cylinders and used to stud the circumference of tumuli. See **haniwa**.

Ki. The ancient name of Mie and Wakayama prefectures. In the Yayoi and Tumulus periods, Ki is thought to have been a strong sea power, often rivaling Kibi in its relations with Yamato. The aged Ki general Oyumi was commissioned by Emperor Yuryaku to attack Silla in AD 465.

Kibi. Ancient name of the region which comprised part of eastern Hiroshima prefecture, Okayama prefecture and a small part of western Hyogo prefecture. It was divided into Kibi Shimotsumichi (western coastal), Kibi Kamitsumichi (east) and Kibi-no-Nakamichi (inland). Kibi was later broken up into Bizen, Bitchu and Bingo, with a later addition of Mimasaka.

Kibi Kamitsumichi. The upper province of Kibi now known as Bizen. Home of King Tasa and his wife, Princess Waka, later wife of Yamato King Yuryaku. Oku and Ushimado are parts of Kibi Kamitsumichi. From a comparison of the size of tumuli, it would appear that Kibi Kamitsumichi was powerful in the late fourth century and again in the late fifth century. Between those times the power lay further west, in central Kibi.

Kibi Miya no Engi. Chronicles of the origins of Kibitsu Shrine.

Kibi-no-Kaja. One of the many names for the demon of Kibi; probably an allusion to the Korean residents of Kibi.

Kibi Shimotsumichi. The province of Kibi, now known as Bitchu and Bingo, or western coastal Kibi. The large island of Kojima was part of Kibi Shimotsumichi. The rebellious King Sakitsuya, who was executed on orders of Emperor Yuryaku, came from this area.

Kibitsu Hiko. See **Isaseri-Hiko-no-Mikoto**.

Kibitsu Jinja. Shrine situated at the entrance to central Kibi on the slopes of Mt Naka. The shrine is dedicated to the spirit and exploits of Prince Kibitsu, one time governor of Kibi. The present buildings were constructed between 1392 and 1427. The Kamaden Hall is of particular significance in the tales of Prince Kibitsu and the demon Ura from Korea.

Kijo (Mt). Location of the Demon's Castle of Kibi. Commands superb lookout points for observation of the south, east and west.

Kimmei. Twenty-ninth king of Japan, reigned AD 540–571. During his reign, Japan lost its position in Korea after Kaya was defeated by Silla in AD 562. Five thousand Korean families migrated to Japan and settled in Kibi and Yamato. Buddhism is also said to have been introduced to Japan in AD 552, but this is probably incorrect, and much earlier.

Kinojo. The castle of the demon of Kibi, located on Mt Kijo.

Kojiki. The first Japanese history compiled by Ono Yasumaro from the recollections of an old woman, Hieda-no-Are. The work was started in AD 711 and finished in AD 712. The *Kojiki* is in three volumes and finishes with the reign of Empress Suiko in AD 628.

Kojima. According to the *Kojiki*, the second island of Japan, after Awaji, created by the gods. Today it is part of Kurashiki City in Okayama prefecture. In the Yayoi and Tumulus periods, Kojima was an enormous island, but now forms a peninsula into the Inland Sea.

Korei. Seventh king of Yamato, Japan (290–215 BC). Father of Isaseri-Hiko-no-Mikoto (Prince Kibitsu).

Kumaso. Barbarian inhabitants of southern Kyushu, said to have descended from a tribe of South Sea immigrants. They were a constant source of irritation to successive Yamato kings over several centuries. They are reputed to have been conquered in the third century by Queen Jingu Kogo, but in all probability were first conquered by the Puyo in the fourth century.

Kunch'ogo. King of Paekche (AD 346–375). Vassal or ally of the Puyo (probably of Puyo descent) who swept through Kaya and onto Japan in AD 369. The seven branch sword presented to the Puyo conqueror of Kaya Wa, inscribed and dated 369, was produced to his order. This sword lies in the Isonokami Shrine in Yamato and was probably the original sword of the Imperial regalia mentioned often in early Japanese histories. Its inscription, date and connection with King Kunch'ogo and Korea are probably the reason for its ultimate rejection.

Kurohime. Kurohime means black princess. The *Nihonshoki* tells of a romance between Kurohime, the daughter of Hata-no-Yashiro-no-Sukune (presumably a Kibi nobleman) and her consequent seduction by the Emperor's brother, Prince Nakatsu. The *Kojiki* refers to Kurohime in the section on the reign of the sixteenth King Nintoku (AD 313–399). Here she is described as a mistress of the king. Her return to Kibi, due to the queen's jealousy, resulted in the king joining her in her native land. A similar story to this is found in the *Nihonshoki* in the section on the fifteenth King Ojin. In this story the emperor refers to her as his spouse. She is said to have been the daughter of Mitomo-Wake, grandson of Prince Kibitsu. She could also have been the wife of King Tasa of Kibi Kamitsumichi—another example of the early historians taking a single character and dividing the life history among many invented characters to pad out the records.

Kyoto. Capital of Japan for over a thousand years. Founded by Emperor Kammu in AD 794.

Kyushu. South-west island of Japan; 420,000 square kilometres in area. Contains the prefectures Fukuoka, Saga, Kumamoto, Oita, Kagoshima and Miyazaki.

Ling Ti. Emperor of the later Han dynasty of China (reigned AD 168–190). Believed to be the ancestor of Achi-no-Omi. The Hata and Aya clans are thought by some to have descended from this Emperor but this error is doubtless caused through deliberate confusion between the Chinese Han dynasty and the Han tribes of Korea. The ideogram of Aya can also be read as Han.

Magatama. Sacred comma-shaped jewel, part of the imperial regalia. They are often found in Jomon and Tumulus period sites, but are rare in the Yayoi period. Their design is probably derived from animal claws. They are also found in Siberia and Korea and have mystical shamanistic properties. They are usually from two to eight centimetres in length, and made from rock crystal, jasper, agate and other stones.

Meiji. Meiji Era (AD 1868–1912). The reign of the one hundred and twenty-second Emperor Mutsuhito.

Mimana. See **Kaya**.

Mimasaka. One of the five districts of Okayama prefecture. Separated from Bizen in AD 713. The largest city in Mimasaka is Tsuyama.

mirrors. Or *kagami* in Japanese, usually bronze. One of the three imperial regalia. Referred to frequently in the ancient histories. In the Yayoi period, mirrors were imported from China and Korea and used as gifts of recognition. They were believed to possess supernatural properties and used to exorcise evil.

Mitomo-Wake. Grandson of Prince Kibitsu and father of Princess Kuro, perhaps the wife of King Ojin. Said to be the ancestor of the nobles of Kaya, in Korea. The *Nihonshoki* tells how Ojin divided up the province of Kibi among Mitomo-Wake's family. This is undoubtedly fictitious but serves to show how important Kibi was to the early Yamato rulers.

Miwa. Region around Mt Miwa, eighteen kilometres from Nara. Thought to be the site of an early dynasty of Yamato rulers.

miyake. A granary or store-house for royal produce, later extended to include land. The *miyake* came to be government offices, for census, records and tax gathering purposes. They were abolished in the Taika reforms of AD 646.

Muraji. A title of honour corresponding to duke. Part of the system of titles brought by the Puyo to Japan in AD 369.

Muromachi. Period between AD 1336–1573.

Mutsu. Ancient province of Aomori prefecture, northern Japan.

Nagayama. Usaburo (1875-1963) local historian of Kurashiki. Compiled the history of Kurashiki in twelve large volumes.

Naka. A hill in central Kibi on the side of which can be found Kibitsu

116

Shrine. On top of the hill are two large tumuli, one which was thought to have been the grave of Prince Kibitsu. Mt Naka is at the entrance to central Kibi and on the east side of the old Sanyo road.

Nara. Prefecture in Yamato. The city of Nara was established in AD 710 and was the first true capital of Japan. It was constructed on the lines of the Chinese Tang capital of Chang An (modern Xian) and around the temples which had been constructed under imperial patronage.

Nichira. A Japanese official in Paekche whose advice was requested by the Emperor Bidatsu on the restoration of Kaya. He travelled to Japan in AD 583 and counselled the emperor. Nichira visited Kibi Kojima on his journey to Yamato. He was assassinated on his return journey to Paekche.

Nihonshoki. Further chronicles of ancient Japan compiled by Ono Yasumaro in AD 720. They cover the period from the first King Jimmu, 660 BC, through to Jito, AD 696. Together with the *Kojiki* this work is the only record of Japan's early history. The two are often at variance in official chronology even though written only eight years apart. It is generally accepted that the two were written to enhance eighth century imperial prestige and bear little record of fact. With careful sifting, however, much of value can be found. Comparison with the Korean histories shows that much of the record of the early Tumulus period is off by two cycles of sixty years. Between the ages of Kings Jimmu and Nintoku seventeen cycles have been interpolated. 'Year One', 660 BC, through to AD 369 (date of the Puyo conquest of Wa) is also within the same seventeen cycles. The first emperor of the Yamato dynasty would most likely have ascended the throne during the seventeenth or eighteenth cycle.

Niigata. Prefecture in northeast Japan, on the Japan Sea.

Obosan. An archaeologically valuable hill cemetery from the late Yayoi period. Situated east of Kurashiki City. The site known as the Kings' Graveyard is thought to have been the burial place of generations of early Kibi chieftains. It was rich in early ceramics and yielded the famous clay cylinder with a model of a house on top. The Tatetsuki ruins are nearby.

Ojin. Fifteenth king of Japan (AD 201–310). He was born in Tsukushi, in northern Kyushu, upon his mother's return from her 'conquest' of Korea. In his reign Achi-no-Omi came to Japan. A three cycle interpolation would place his reign neatly with that of the Puyo conquest of AD 369. He was probably a Puyo leader and the deeds of his mother have been reversed for the sake of later eighth century imperial prestige.

Okayama. Prefecture in western Japan, facing the Inland Sea. Encompasses Bizen, Bitchu, eastern Bingo and Mimasaka provinces, all part of the ancient Kibi kingdom. Okayama City is the prefectural capital.

Okinoshima. A sacred island off the coast of Fukuoka where women are prohibited to set foot. Recent archaeological discoveries have revealed Middle Eastern, Persian, Indian and Chinese artifacts of ancient origin. These include armour,

swords, spears, looms and pottery. Okinoshima was a sacred shrine and stopping place on journeys from and to Korea. It was probably first used by Koreans on their journeys to trade, immigrate and conquer in the early centuries AD. Many Korean artifacts found on Okinoshima have identical parallels with objects discovered in tumuli in Kibi.

Oku. An area in eastern Kibi rich in tumuli of the fourth and fifth centuries. The great Sue kilns of Samukaze are in Oku. These kilns later moved to Imbe, where the famous Bizen stoneware is still created.

Omi (title). A hereditary court noble and, together with Muraji, one of the two highest titles. Persons or families bearing this title participated in the running of the Yamato court and often acted as ambassadors and provincial governors.

omphalos. The navel, or central point, of a system. The discovery of a strange omphalos stone at the Tatetsuki Shrine in Kibi suggests that Tatetsuki and nearby Obosan were the nucleus points of ancient Kibi.

Ono Yasumaro. Descended from King Jimmu and was commissioned in AD 711 to write down the first history of Japan in three volumes from the memory of Hieda-no-Are, a woman with a superior intellect. Ono Yasumaro also assisted in the compilation of the *Nihonshoki* in AD 720. His grave, containing a cinerary box with an inscription, was discovered about twenty years ago, near Nara.

O-sora. A member of the Kibi Shimotsumichi bowman's guild who served at Emperor Yuryaku's court in Yamato. The *Nihonshoki* credits him with the exposure of the treachery of King Sakitsuya of Kibi.

Osumi. Peninsular part of Kagoshima prefecture in south Kyushu.

Paekche. An ancient kingdom of southwest Korea known by the Japanese as Kudara. The name Paekche probably derives from a Manchurian Puyo migrant group which founded the Kingdom in the early centuries AD. Most, if not all, of Japan's cultural heritage stems from Paekche and its Manchurian Puyo founders. The earliest Japanese histories go to great lengths to distort fact and in several places suggest that Japan conquered Paekche in AD 200. Paekche was the most faithful ally and was rewarded with disdain after its defeat by Silla in AD 663. This Japanese disdain and characteristic xenophobia is best seen in the deliberate twists, cover-ups and distortions of truth written in the *Kojiki* and *Nihonshoki* in the early eighth century— only fifty years after the fall of Paekche.

Puyo. Puyo tribes migrated south from their home in the fertile river deltas of eastern-central Manchuria in the early Christian era. Paekche in western Korea presumably takes its name from one of the groups which migrated south, gradually seizing control of the tribes in their path. The Puyo were horsemen, ruled by a warrior elite, and kept slaves. By the mid-fourth century, the Puyo had conquered all the important western tribes of southern Korea and the peninsular Wa kingdoms. In AD 369 they moved onto 'Japan' Wa, conquering the kingdoms as they moved eastwards. Their kings probably ruled Japan from different places, including Kibi, from AD 369 until the mid-sixth century. The roots of the present Japanese imperial dynasty have their origins in Manchuria.

Ritchu. Seventeenth king of Japan (reigned AD 400–405), son of King Nintoku, according to the *Kojiki* and *Nihonshoki*. Probably never existed and was invented as a stopgap by the compilers of the early histories.

Ritsuryo. A collection of civil and criminal codes specifying the accepted norms of behaviour and punishment. Issued in AD 670, they were superseded by the Taiho codes of AD 701.

Sakitsuya. King of Kibi Shimotsumichi, who rebelled against Yamato King Yuryaku (AD 457–479) and was executed.

San In. The area encompassing Shimane, Tottori and part of Yamaguchi and Okayama prefectures. See **Chugoku**.

Sanyodo. Literally, 'exposed mountain region', but commonly used as a term to denote the road from the east (Yamato) to the west (Kyushu). The Sanyodo passed through Kibi close to the Kibitsu Shrine and Ashimori Town.

Seinei. Twenty-second king of Japan (reigned AD 480–484). His half-brother, Prince Hoshikawa (whose mother came from Kibi) became pretender to the throne upon the death of their father, King Yuryaku.

Shi. King Shi of Wa, for whom the seven-branch sword mentioned in the *Nihonshoki* (now kept in the Isonokami Shrine in Yamato) was made. Shi was, in all probability, a Puyo conqueror of Japan Wa in AD 369, the date which is inlaid upon the sword.

Shinkansen. Railway for special high speed trains, which commenced service in 1964 between Tokyo and Osaka. The line was later extended on through Okayama (Kibi) and later still to Kyushu.

Shiraino *miyake*. Shiraino has no precise meaning. Literally translated it reads 'white boar', which is obscure and meaningless. The ancient Japanese used Chinese ideographs phonetically. There might well be several alternative pronounciations for the combination of 'white boar'. Similarly, the word 'Miyake' comprising two characters is confusing although the second ideograph means a granary or storehouse which may relate in some way to the role of the office implied. The Shiraino *miyake* were probably Yamato designed centers for control of outlying areas. They were also thought to be district centers for government. The *Nihonshoki* has the arrogance to suggest that the Korean kingdoms of Paekche and Silla were under the umbrella of 'Miyake' or Shiraino *miyake*. There is the possibility that Shiraino *miyake* were power control centers over possible Kayan nationalism in Kibi and elsewhere. The *miyake* were, however, granaries to which were attached cultivated lands and serfs and

the origin of the term could well be derived from the appointment of later immigrant people from Kaya as serfs and menials within a modification of the earlier *be* (see *Be*) or guild system. It is interesting to note that wherever Shiraino *miyake* were thought to have been positioned, Buddhist temples were built on the sites (another form of control over the people.) Iron works are also to be found at such places which clearly indicates the continual Yamato obsession with Kibi's wealth through iron and the dangers associated with the possession of such valuable raw resources without proper Yamato supervision.

Shodoshima. Shodoshima is the second-largest island in the Inland Sea. Often mentioned in the first histories as a stopping place on journeys between Yamato and Kibi, which indicates clearly the shipping lanes of the early centuries (ie., via Kibi).

Silla. Shiragi in Japanese; one of the ancient kingdoms of Korea. Silla was the habitual enemy of Yamato which, throughout the early centuries AD, sent forces to aid the other Korean kingdoms of Paekche and Kaya.

Sogo Iname. Minister under Emperors Senkwa (AD 536–539) and Kimmei (AD 540–571). The *Nihonshoki* states that Buddhism was introduced to Japan in 552 AD upon the introduction and gift of Buddhist statues from the King of Paekche. These gifts were passed to Iname by the emperor who, after opposition from the old chieftains of Yamato, thought experimentation with the new doctrines would be best for all. Iname erected a Buddhist shrine at his house, which was called Kogen-ji.

Soga Umako. Son of Soga Iname; prime minister. Established the Shiraino *miyake* in Kibi. Iname was head of all the Korean families in Japan, the implication being that Kibi, with a huge immigrant Korean population, would have prospered under Soga protection. It is interesting to note that Kibi power dwindled after the death of Umako in AD 626.

Soja. Small city north of Kurashiki City in central Okayama (Kibi). Site of many important Yayoi and Tumulus period ruins.

Sue. High fired ceramics produced in Japan and Korea from the fourth century AD. This style of pottery was introduced to Japan from Korea, probably by the Puyo, in the late fourth century. Sue techniques were originally Chinese in origin and were probably assimilated by the Puyo in their migrations southward. It is thought that the introduction of the tunnel kiln to Japan took place at the same time. Sue ware was manufactured by a guild of potters who specialized in ceremonial ware for use in burials. Large quantities of Sue are unearthed frequently from Tumulus period graves. Generally, Sue ware is undecorated, although in Kibi, some pieces are found with fine incised designs, as are numerous pieces showing a specialized use of spatulas during the throwing process. In Kibi, the same kilns were later used for the manufacture of tiles. There is a very close similarity in style between Kaya high-fired ceramics and those made in Kibi, and it is possible that the new techniques may have been first attempted in Kibi and north Kyushu, spreading eastward.

Sujin. Tenth king of Japan (97–30 BC). Cycle adjusted date of death AD 258 or 318. Dispatched Kibitsu Hiko to conquer Kibi and pacify Izumo. The early histories tell that during his reign the first embassy from Kaya arrived in Japan.

Tabe. Guild farmers who, in some cases, worked for the *miyake* in Kibi.

Takahashi. Important river of Kibi to the west of Kurashiki City. The delta between the Takahashi and Asahi rivers is rich in Tumulus period tombs. The southern stretches of the river have changed their course over the centuries. The river flows into the Inland Sea at Tamashima.

Takatsuki. Sue stoneware bowls on tall pedestal feet.

Tamba. Province with districts in Kyoto and Hyogo Prefectures in Yamato.

Tasa. King of Kibi Kamitsumichi, whose wife married King Yuryaku (AD 457–478). Tasa was exiled to Kaya by Yuryaku as governor, where he fermented relations between the Yamato Court and Paekche.

Temmu. Fortieth emperor of Japan (reigned AD 673–686).

Tempyo. Period corresponding to AD 722–748.

tokan. *Hajiki* clay coffins; are peculiar to Kibi and often elaborately carved. They were produced in the *haji* style (open firing); found in eastern Kibi. Sue *tokan* are more common and found in wide areas outside of Kibi. *Tokan* are often found together with stone coffins in later sixth century sites.

Tokushima. Prefecture in northeast Shikoku; capital with the same name. The treacherous Naruto Straits are nearby, with whirlpools. Awaji Island separates Tokushima from Ki and Yamato.

tokushu kidai. Large pottery cylinders produced in Kibi at the end of the Yayoi period. The cylinders were often well decorated with incised geometric designs, cut out patterns and bands. Used for offerings at cemeteries.

Toma. Mysterious vassal kingdom of Yamatai, mentioned in the Chinese Wei Chih chronicles. Population was said to be forty thousand households. Location is unknown but thought to be somewhere along the Inland Sea, possibly in Kibi.

tsubo. Unit of measurement equaling 3.3 square metres. One *tsubo* is divisible by two *jo* (2.5 square metres), the measurement of tatami mats.

Tsukushi. In ancient times, the term meant the whole of the island of Kyushu. Generally, it applies to the name of Fukuoka prefecture. Tsukushi is thought to have had very strong relations with Korea and China.

Tsushima. Valuable archaeological site in Okayama City, where many Yayoi period remains have been found. The earliest discovered rice paddies in Kibi were found at Tsushima and preserved.

Tsuyama. Largest city in Mimasaka, northern Kibi.

uji. Title or office implying the head or senior branch of a family. In the Tumulus period this term (introduced by the Puyo) denoted senior rank.

Uneme. Female palace attendants, usually the daughters of local governors, chosen for their beauty and cultural talents.

Ura. Another name for the legendary demon of Kibi.

Wa. Term used by the Chinese in the chronicles of Wei (Wei Chih) to describe the kingdoms of southern Korea and Japan. Wa, in Chinese, meant 'the land(s) of dwarfs'. Japanese Wa was most likely controlled as a series of branch states from Kaya in south Korea. The term is used widely in the early histories of both Korea and Japan and the name was later corrupted to Yamato.

Wei Chih. Chinese chronicles written in the third century describing the land of Wa (Japan). The Japanese term for the chronicles is Gishi Wa Jin Den.

Yamaguchi. The westernmost prefecture of Honshu, culturally influenced by Tsukushi rather than Kibi and Yamato.

Yamatai (koku). An ancient Japanese 'Wa' Kingdom referred to in detail in the third century AD Chinese history the Wei-Chih or chronicles of Wei. The actual location of this mysterious kingdom has yet to be determined. The details of Yamatai and its mysterious Queen Himeko as described by the Chinese, have tantalized archaeologists and historians for centuries.

Yamato. The collective name for the five provinces of Yamato. The characters used to write the name are a corruption of the Chinese name Wa, used in the Wei-Chih chronicles, meaning 'the land of dwarfs'.

Yayoi. Term used to describe the period in Japanese history corresponding to c. 400 BC–AD 250. The term and dates are very loose, as different parts of the country changed culturally at different times. The name was coined after a site in Tokyo where the earliest pottery examples of the ancient culture were discovered and properly studied.

Yoshii River. One of the three great rivers of Kibi. Situated in eastern Okayama prefecture in the area once known as Kibi Kamitsumichi, now Bizen.

Yuga (Mt). Important Yayoi site on Kibi Kojima, where *dotaku* and ceremonial swords have been discovered.

Yuryaku. Twenty-first king of Japan (AD 457–479). Despot. Married a Kibi princess who had previously been the wife of King Tasa of Kibi Kamitsumichi. He encouraged Korean artisans to come and settle in Japan. Upon his death, a coup d'état was attempted by his son, whose mother was the Princess Waka of Kibi. Yuryaku was ultimately succeeded by his chosen heir, Seimei, who died after a reign of five years.

BIBLIOGRAPHY

Acta Asiatica
  Bulletin of the Institute of Eastern Culture,
  The Toho Gakkai, Tokyo, vol. 31 (1977), 34 (1978).
Anesaki Masaharu
  History of Japanese Religion, 1930. Reprinted by Tuttle,
  Rutland, Vermont 1971.
Aston, W.G. (trsl.)
  Nihongi; Chronicles of Japan From the Earliest Times to
  AD, *697.* 1896. Reprinted by Tuttle, Rutland, Vermont
  1972.
Chamberlain, Basil Hall *(tr.) Ko-ji-ki; Records of Ancient*
  Matters, 1883. Reprinted by   The Asiatic Society of Japan,
  Tokyo 1973.
Doi Takuji and Sato Yoneji
  Nippon no Minzuoku Okayama; Daiichi Hoki Shuppan
  Kaisha, Tokyo 1972.
Domon Ken, Serizawa Chosuke and Tsuboi Kiyotari
  Nipponjin no Genzo, Heibonsha, Tokyo 1966.
Egami Namio
  Kiba Minzoku Kokka; Chuo Koronsha, Tokyo 1967.
  The Beginnings of Japanese Art, Heibonsha, Tokyo 1973.
Ezakai T.; Serizawa Chosuke and Sakatsumi S.
  Nippon Kokogaku Shojiten, New Science Sha,
  Tokyo 1983.
Fujii Shun
  Kibitsu Jinja, Nippon Bunkyo Shuppan, Okayama 1964.
Godonenkan Bessatsu
  Kibi 2600 Nenshi, Godo Shinbunsha, Okayama 1939.
Han Woo-keun
  The History of Korea, The Eul-Yoo Publishing, Seoul 1970.
Kamamoto Yoshimasa
  Okayama no Kofun, Nippon Bunkyo Shuppan, Okayama
  1964.
Kanno Tsutomu
  Rekishi no Tabi Kibi, Akita Shoten, Tokyo 1971.
  Kibiji, Nippon Bunkyo Shuppan, Okayama 1967.
Katsura Matasaburo
  Okayama no Yakimono, Nippon Bunkyo Shuppan,
  Okayama 1964.
Kidder, J. Edward
  Japan Before Buddhism, Thames and Hudson, London
  1959.
Kim, J.
  Kankoku no Iseki O Horu, Gakusesha, Tokyo 1981.
Kim, John K.
  Korean Art Seen Through Museums, Eastern Media,
  Seoul 1979.
Kim, T.
  Nippon no Naka no Chosen Bunka, Kodansha, Tokyo
  1979.
Kinojo Gakjitsu and Chusai Inkai
  Kinojo, Sanyo Insatsu K. K., Okayama 1980.

Koyama Fujio
  Bizen Yaki, Nippon Bunkyo Shuppan, Okayama 1970.
Kusumoto Kenkichi & Nakamura Akio
  Kurashiki Fubutsushi, Asahi Shinbunsha, Tokyo 1972.
Ledyard, Gari
  'Galloping Along With The Horseriders: Looking For The
  Founders of Japan', *Journal of Japanese Studies,* Colombia
  University 1974.
Mainichi Shinbun
  Kibiji Sanyo-do, Mainichi Shinbunsha, Tokyo 1972.
Makabe Tadahiko and Yoshiko
  Kodai Kibi Okoku no Nazo, Shin Jinbutsu Oraisha,
  Tokyo 1972.
  Kibi Kodaishi no Michi o Toku, Shin Jinbutsu Oraisha,
  Tokyo 1981.
  Kibiji Kodaishi no Fuke, Iwanami Shoten, Tokyo 1983.
  Okayama no Iseki Meguri, Nippon Bunkyo Shuppan,
  Okayama 1970.
Mishina Akihide
  Nippon no Rekishi (Vol. 2); Shinwa no Sekai Shueisha,
  Tokyo 1974.
Miyake Chiaki
  Kurashiki no Kantaku; Kurashiki City Education
  Department, Kurashiki 1976.
Mizuno Y.
  Nihon Kodai no Kokka Keisei, Kodansha, Tokyo 1967.
Nagayama Usaburo *Kurashiki Shi Shi* (Vols. 1 to 12); Meicho
  Shuppan, Kurashiki 1973.
Nishikaya Hiroshi
  Okayama to Chosen, Nippon Bunkyo Shuppan,
  Okayama 1982.
Oba Hiromichi
  Dotaku no Nazo; Kobunsha, Tokyo 1974.
Okada A., Toyota Takeshi and Wakamori T.
  Nippon no Rekishi, Yomiuri Shinbunsha, Tokyo 1959.
Ono Sokyo
  Shinto: The Kami Way, Tuttle, Rutland, Vermont 1962.
Papinot, E. *Historical & Geographical Dictionary of Japan,*
  1910. Reprinted by Tuttle, Rutland, Vermont 1972.
Philippi, Donald (trsl.)
  Kojiki, University of Tokyo Press, Tokyo 1968.
Sanyo Shinbun Sha
  Kibiji, Sanyo Shinbun Sha, Okayama 1971.
Sekaibunkasha
  Nippontanjo, Sekaibunkasha, Tokyo 1967.
Tateishi Noritoshi
  Okayama no Densetsu, Nippon Bunkyo Shuppan,
  Okayama 1967.
Whitney Hall, John
  Japan from Pre-History to Modern Times, Tuttle,
  Rutland, Vermont 1971.

INDEX

A
Achi 86, 88, 89, 102
Ajiki 102
Akada (Temple) 109
animism 33
Ankan (Emperor) 2, 90
Aomori (Prefecture) 3
aristocracy 59, 68, 70, 83, 100, 104
Asahi (River) 6, 7, 9, 21, 36, 38, 44, 50, 52,
      56, 85, 94
Ashi 9, 44, 89
Ashida (River) 9
Ashimori (River) 9, 44, 52, 77, 85
Ashimori (Town) 118
Asuka (Period) 92, 106, 113
Awaji 63, 113, 116, 119
axe head 56
Aya 86, 89, 113, 114, 115, 116

B
bells 33, 64, 73, 85
Bidatsu (Emperor) 91, 101, 103
Bingo Province 2, 3, 9, 10, 14, 20, 41, 91,
      96, 98, 106
Bitchu Province 2, 41, 47, 50, 86, 96, 100
Bizen Kojima 2
Bizen Province 92, 100
bronze 12, 14, 15, 17, 18, 20, 31, 32, 33,
      36, 41, 53, 56, 70, 73, 102, 103
Bu (King Yuryaku) 58, 83, 114
Buddhism 100, 101, 102, 103, 104, 106

C
castle(s) 74, 75, 76, 77, 78, 81, 85, 116
Central Government 6, 90, 92, 101
chieftains 48, 52, 56, 59, 62, 63, 66, 71,
    78, 83, 85, 95, 100, 102, 103, 104, 109
Chin (King Hanzei) 58, 59, 87, 101, 114
China 14, 20, 33, 41, 47, 48, 58, 59,
      68, 82, 89, 101, 116, 119
Chokkomon 62
Chugoku 15, 98
clan(s) 15, 32, 33, 38, 47, 59, 60, 71, 78,
      83, 84, 94, 102, 103, 104, 106
clowns 73
cock rooster 70
coffin(s) 26, 31, 53, 92, 95, 96, 98, 100

Confucianism 102
conscription 68
costume 71
crown(s) 66, 70
Cultural Agency 6

D
death (dead) 2, 27, 32, 47, 58, 64, 65, 66,
      76, 77, 81, 82, 100, 103
demon 76, 78, 84, 114
dotaku 14, 15, 17, 18, 20, 31

E
Engishiki 98
Etsu 35, 38

F
fishermen 48, 68, 113
Fukuda 9, 17
Fukuyama 14, 15, 29, 113
Funao 9
fundo 17, 18, 20, 114
funeral(s) 27, 65, 106

G
GemmYO (Empress) 2
general(s) 6, 31, 36, 41, 52, 65, 66, 76,
      82, 83
Genkai Strait 12, 56, 63
gold 32, 70, 87, 88, 92
Gotan ruins 106
grave(s) 27, 29, 35, 38, 44, 53, 82, 109
guilds (Be) 68, 85

H
Hakuho Period 31, 106, 114
Han 32, 53, 86, 89
Handayama 6, 38
haniwa 26, 29, 32, 38, 41, 44, 45, 52, 71, 78
Hanzei (King) 48, 58, 59
Harima (Channel) 14, 35
Hashima 91
Hata 85, 86, 89, 103, 104
Hayashi (Lin) 84, 85
Himiko (Queen) 3, 29, 32, 36
Hirafuku 100
Hiroshima 2, 14, 15, 17, 98
Hoita 31, 100
Honshu 85
horse(s) 56, 60, 70, 78, 80

horsemen 80, 82, 88
Hoshikawa (Prince 65, 66, 82, 90, 91

I
Ifuku 6
Imperial Household Agency 45, 56, 58, 82
Inland Sea 2, 7, 9, 12, 14, 15, 17, 18, 20,
    21, 31, 44, 47, 50, 73, 81, 85, 90, 109
iron 7, 10, 12, 14, 21, 33, 53, 56, 59, 73,
    74, 84, 85, 87, 90, 91, 95, 98, 104,
Isonokami Shrine 87, 88
Iwakura 9
Iyobeyama 26

J
Japan Sea 50, 106
Jimmu (King) 87
Jomon Period 7, 9, 17
Joto 21, 76
Jotoshiki 21, 26

K
kadota 9
Kagawa Prefecture 14, 15, 31
Kamaden 78
Kanakurayama (Tomb) 56, 70, 95
Kara (Kaya) 86
Kawachi 50, 60, 96
Kaya 48, 58, 59, 64, 65, 66, 70, 76, 80, 81,
  83, 85, 86, 87, 88, 89, 91, 92, 94, 103, 104
Keiko (Emperor) 35, 45, 50
Ki Province 65, 66, 76, 83
Kibi 2, 3, 7, 9, 10, 12, 14, 15, 17, 18, 20,
    21, 25, 26, 27, 29, 31, 32, 33, 35, 36, 38, 41,
    44, 45, 47, 48, 50, 52, 53, 56, 58, 59,
    60, 62, 63, 64, 65, 66, 68, 70, 71, 73,
    74, 75, 76, 77, 78, 80, 81, 82, 83, 84,
    85, 86, 88, 89, 90, 91, 92, 94, 95, 98,
    100, 101, 102, 103, 104, 106, 109
Kibitsu Jinja 44
Kimmei (Emperor) 2, 83, 90, 102, 103
Kinai 12, 14, 15, 17, 18, 20, 21, 22, 26, 29,
    32, 35, 38, 41, 44, 45, 47, 48, 50, 52,
    53, 59, 60, 62, 63, 70, 98
Ko (King Ankyo) 58
Kobayashi (Professor) 36
Kojiki 2, 35, 41, 59, 62, 74, 86, 87, 88, 101
Kojima 2, 12, 14, 15, 17, 44, 45, 47, 89,
    90, 91, 92, 94,

Komorizuka (Temple) 96, 98
Komorizuka (Tomb) 96, 98
Korea 7, 12, 14, 15, 33, 36, 41, 44, 45, 47,
    48, 56, 59, 60, 63, 64, 65, 66, 68, 70,
    71, 76, 80, 82, 83, 84, 86, 87, 89, 91, 94
Korei (Emperor) 35, 41
Koryuji (Temple) 106
Kumo 106
Kuni 84
Kurashiki 2, 9, 12, 20, 21, 26, 29, 45, 52,
    85, 89, 92, 96, 100
Kurumazuka 36, 38, 41, 52
Kyoto 29, 36, 106
Kyushu 7, 12, 14, 15, 17, 18, 20, 26, 33, 44,
    45, 47, 48, 58, 62, 63, 68, 73, 81, 85

L
Lin (Hayashi) 84, 85

M
magatama 70, 73
Makabe 52
Manchuria 78, 80, 84
Masu 90
Meiji 6
military 6, 41, 60, 68, 73, 80, 81, 85
Mimasaka 3, 10, 91, 95, 98, 100, 106
mirror(s) 32, 36, 38, 73, 86, 87, 88, 89
Miyake 90, 91, 92, 94, 98, 100, 101, 103, 106
Miyoshi 10, 106
Muromachi 35, 44

N
Naka (Mount) 44, 45, 76, 78
Nara 29, 32, 38, 44, 70, 73, 85, 86, 87, 106
National Museum, Tokyo 53, 56
Nihonshoki 2, 3, 35, 41, 45, 48, 62, 63, 64,
    66, 74, 80, 84, 86, 87, 88, 89, 90, 91,
    94, 98, 101, 102
Niigata 3
Niiyama 76, 84, 85, 104
Nintoku (Emperor) 2, 48, 50, 58, 60, 62, 80,
    81, 87, 94
Numa 10

O
Obosan 29, 31, 32, 33, 38, 78
Ojin (king) 48, 50, 58, 60, 62, 74, 82, 86, 94
Okayama City 6, 7, 9, 26, 35, 36, 44, 86,
    95, 106

Okayama Prefecture 2
Okayama University 38
Okinoshima 56
omphalos 78

P
Pada (Hata) 85
Paekche 58, 59, 65, 70, 76, 80, 83, 84, 85,
    86, 87, 88, 91, 92, 101, 102, 103, 106
pilots 14, 48
potters 21, 68, 84, 96
pottery 6, 7, 9, 15, 21, 26, 27, 29, 31, 38,
    41, 56, 70, 71, 95, 98, 100, 104
Puyo 58, 74, 76, 78, 80, 81, 82, 83, 84,
    85, 86, 87, 88, 89, 91, 94, 100, 101, 102,
    103, 104, 106, 109

R
Ritchiu (King) 48, 50, 58, 60, 82
Ritchu (King) 48, 50, 58, 60, 82
royal families 68
Ryoguzan 50, 53

S
Sai (King Ingyo) 58
Saidaiji 9
Sakakiyama (Tomb) 56, 58, 70
Sakitsuya (King) 63, 64, 66, 84
Sakuzan 50, 52, 81
San (King Nintoku) 17, 58, 81
Seinei (King) 53, 65, 66, 82, 84
Seno 9
Senzoku (Tomb) 62
shaman, shamanism 17, 21, 70, 78, 104
shell mounds 9, 47, 50
Shi (King) 87, 88, 89
Shiba Tatto 104
Shibukawa 9
Shikoku 15, 47, 50, 98
Shimaji 9
Shimane 29, 106
Shinto 70, 78
Shionasu 9
Shiraino 98, 100, 101, 103, 106
Sho 9
Shoda (Temple) 109
Shodoshima (Shodo Island) 14, 63
Soga 90, 91, 101, 102, 103, 104, 106, 109
Soja (City) 26, 27, 44, 47, 50, 85, 86, 96, 104

soldiers 64, 73, 76
Sugo 90
Suinin (King) 76, 78
Sumatah 104
sun 18, 33, 70, 87
Sungari 78
Sungari (River) 78
Sushin 35, 78, 103, 104
sword(s) 14, 15, 17, 32, 64, 73, 86, 87, 88, 89

T
Taisanjo 83
Takahashi River 9, 45, 74
talisman 18, 20, 70
Tamba 3, 35
Tanematsuyama 12, 14
Tasa (King) 64, 65, 66
tatami 94, 95
Tatetsuki ruins 76, 78
Terado (Temple) 106
Terayama 52, 104
Todaiji (Temple) 85
Totsuki 38, 41, 52
traders 14
tsubo 26
Tsukinowa (Tomb) 95
Tsukuriyama 31, 50, 52, 56, 58, 62, 98
Tsuyama 10, 91, 95
tumuli 29, 31, 32, 33, 36, 38, 44, 45, 47,
    50, 52, 53, 56, 59, 60, 62, 68, 70, 71,
    75, 81, 82, 89, 90, 91, 92, 95, 100,
    102, 104, 109
Tumulus Period 2, 22, 27, 29, 32, 36, 38,
    41, 60, 94, 95, 96, 98, 100
Uji 71, 84
Ushimado 44, 47, 53

W
Wa 3, 48, 58, 59, 60, 66, 68, 70, 80, 81,
    83, 85, 87, 88, 89, 101, 103
weavers 63, 68, 84, 85, 89, 102

Y
Yagui (Shrine) 77, 78
Yakage 26, 27
Yamaguchi 15, 17, 98
Yamatai(koku) 3, 22, 29
Yamato 2, 3, 12, 14, 15, 17, 18, 20, 21,

22, 26, 29, 32, 35, 36, 38, 41, 44, 45,
47, 48, 50, 52, 53, 58, 59, 60, 62, 63,
64, 65, 66, 68, 70, 75, 76, 77, 80, 81,
82, 83, 84, 85, 86, 88, 89, 90, 91, 92,
94, 96, 98, 100, 101, 102, 103, 104, 109

Yashima 45

Yayoi 5, 6, 7, 9, 10, 12, 14, 15, 17, 18, 20,
21, 26, 27, 29, 31, 32, 33, 36, 38, 44,
47, 52, 70, 73, 74, 83, 90

Yoshii River 7, 53

Yunnan 16

ACKNOWLEDGEMENTS

I would like to express my great appreciation to the following for their assistance and indispensable contributions in the completion of this work:

Mr Masahiro Miyake of the Kurashiki City offices, for his help over so many years in finding answers to my many questions and allowing me access to his library.

The Kurashiki Archaeological Museum and the curators for their patience (and sometimes lack of it). Particularly, Mr and Mrs T. Makabe, whose research, writing and format have been my model and invaluable in the early chapters concerning the Yayoi and Tumulus periods.

The librarian and staff of the Kurashiki Municipal Library, who made rare documents available and spent considerable time seeking references and copying them.

My wife Mizue, on whose shoulders fell the real task of the translation of the numerous complicated Japanese language reference works.

Mr John Cousins, without whose kind guidance, enthusiasm and hours of editing this would never have been started and certainly, without the help of Mr Christopher Frape and the patient publisher, never completed.

A very special thanks to Mrs Andrew Caldecott for ironing out so many of the bumps. Also to Georg Fr. Händel who kept me sane during my studies.

While the manuscript was in preparation, my father, Eric Frederic Gorman, my Japanese sponsor and mentor, Mayor Shigeki Oyama of Kurashiki City, and Sir John Pilcher, former British ambassador to Japan, a kind friend, father figure and constant source of encouragement, died. To their memory, I dedicate this volume. The author's and photographer's proceeds from this work will be donated to the Shigeki Oyama Foundation for the encouragement of international exchanges of handicapped young people.

BIOGRAPHICAL NOTES

MICHAEL S.F. GORMAN was born in Christchurch, New Zealand and educated at Waihi School Winchester and Christ´s College. He has been a resident of Japan for over thirty years and instigated the Christchurch-Kurashiki sister city link, which was the first between New Zealand and Japan. Gorman has been a weekly art columnist for the Japan Times and Yomiuri newspapers. He has written numerous articles on oriental ceramics for international journals. He lives in Kurashiki City with his wife, Mizue.

AKIO NAKAMURA was born in Kurashiki City, Japan. He studied photography under the legendary Yoichi Midorikawa. Nakamura is one of Japan´s foremost nature photographers. His work has been widely published and he has won many Japanese awards. His work has also been exhibited internationally.